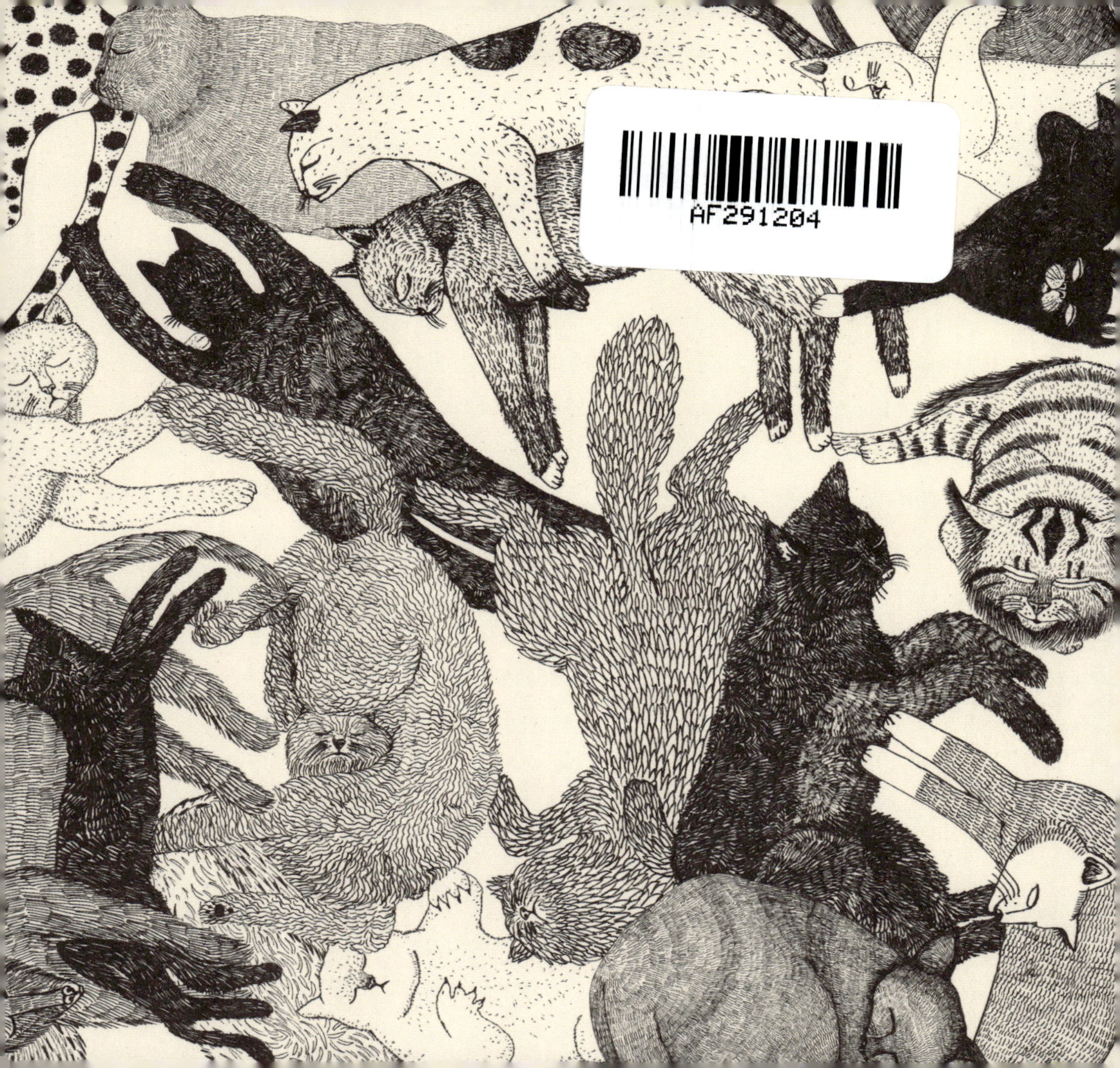
AF291204

...wouldn't it make a
Siamese cat laugh?

James Joyce, *Ulysses*

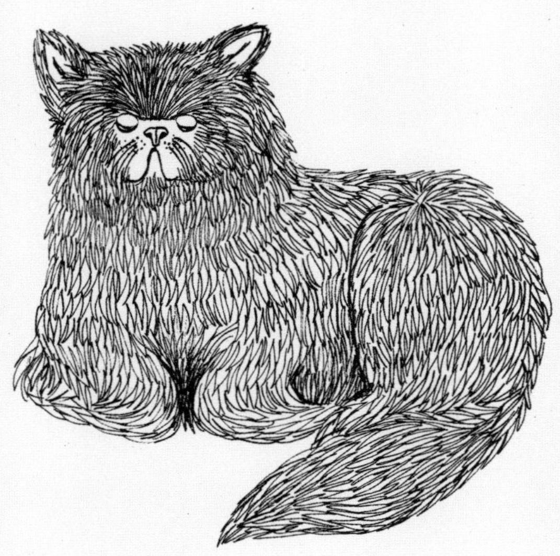

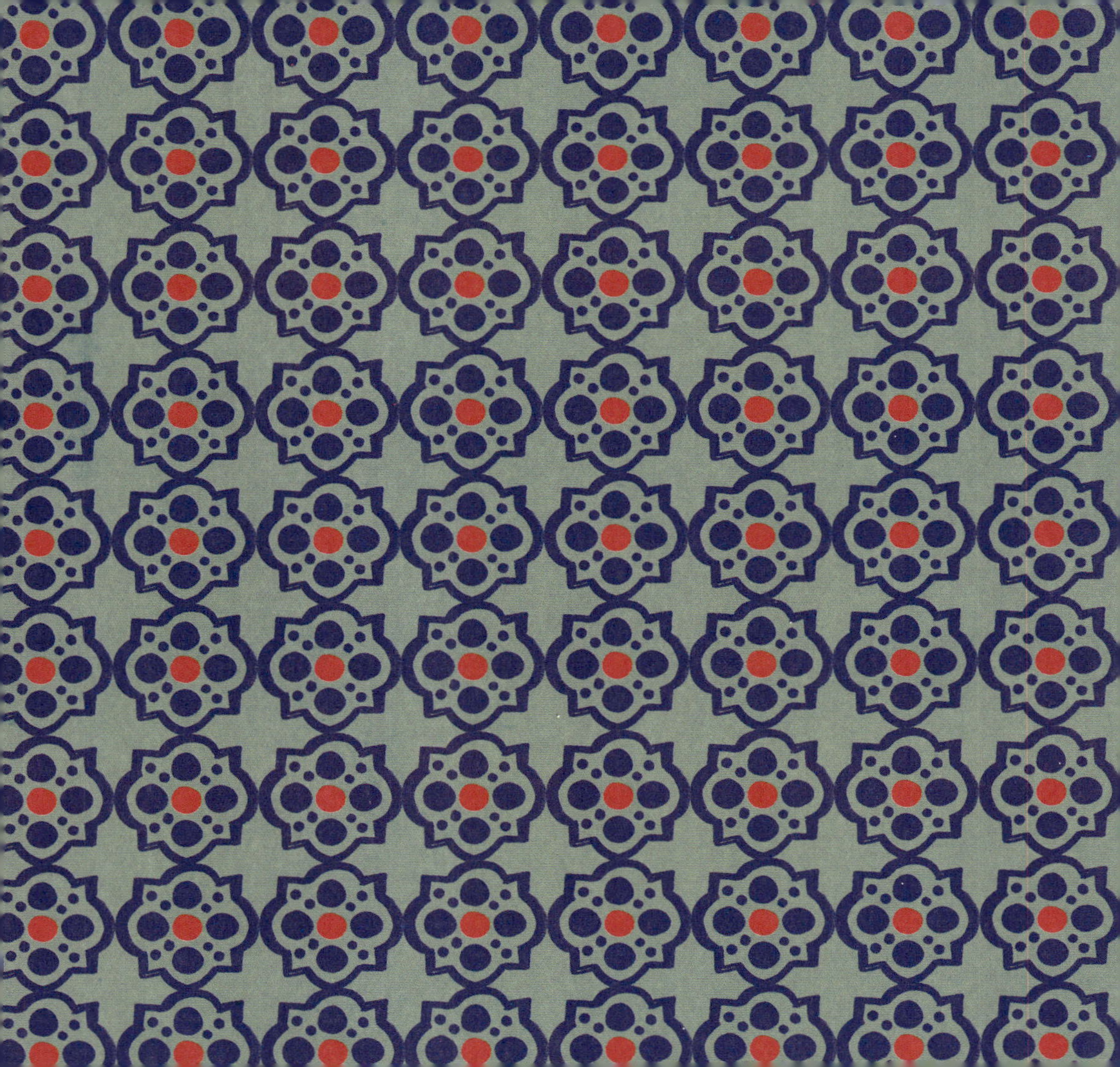

Cat Naps

The secret life of cats

Przemysław Wechterowicz

Illustrations by Kasia Walentynowicz

Original English translation by Antonia Lloyd-Jones

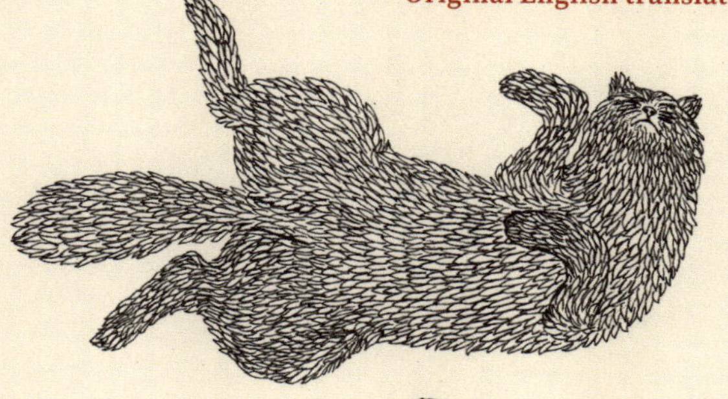

BOOK HOUSE
a SALARIYA imprint

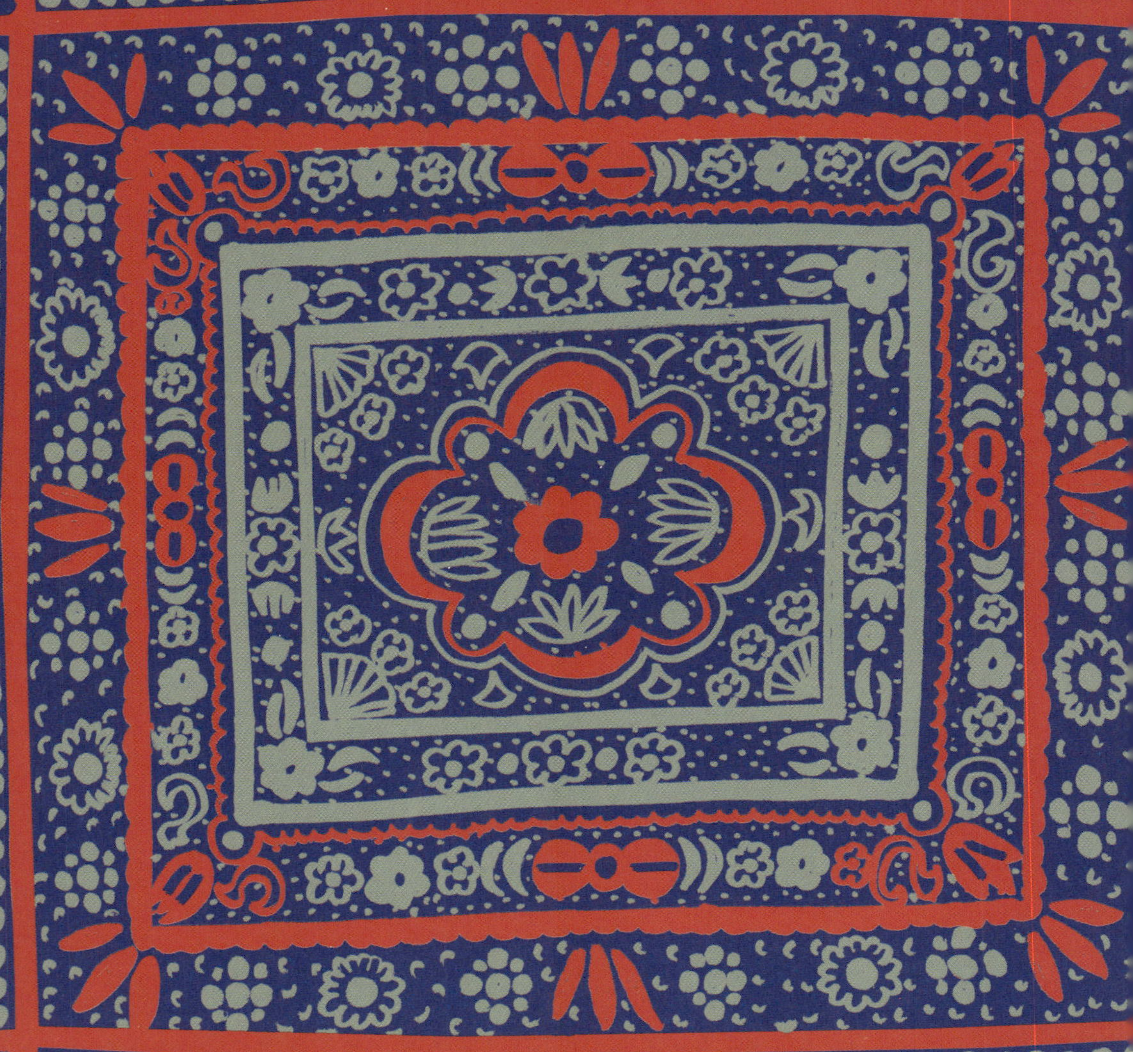

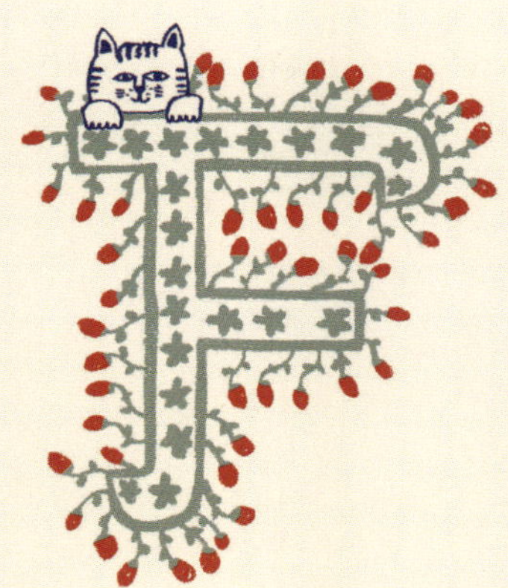

or a beginner cat at the start of your career, this is the perfect book for you. We have pooled the experiences of thousands of past generations of felines. Through their unstinting efforts, sometimes lasting for days and nights, they have managed over the centuries to perfect the art of sleeping. You were made to snooze, catnap and snore, so have a good stretch and a yawn to get your mojo working. Now spread out on a suitable tree branch, sofa, or a nice comfy bed to try out some of the positions shown in this little catnapping manual. Consult it on a regular basis and you'll soon master the art of choosing the best spot and pose for a comfy sleep.

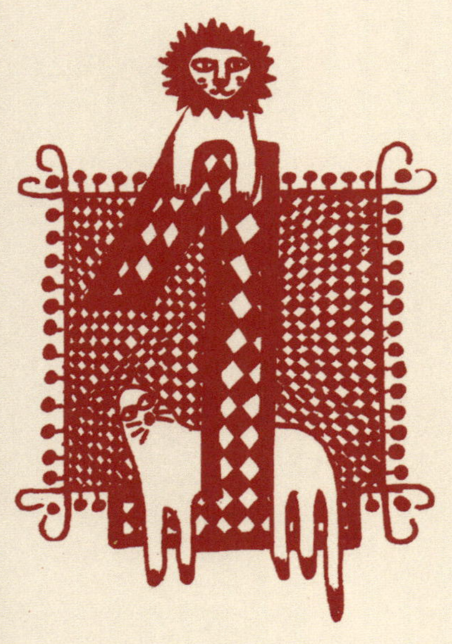

Life is very busy, y'know,
Such a lot to do.
Balls of wool need chasing, y'know,
And mice need hunting, too.

Once I've eaten my breakfast, y'know,
I really need a rest.
You must make room on the bed, y'know,
I need to grab some zzzzz's!

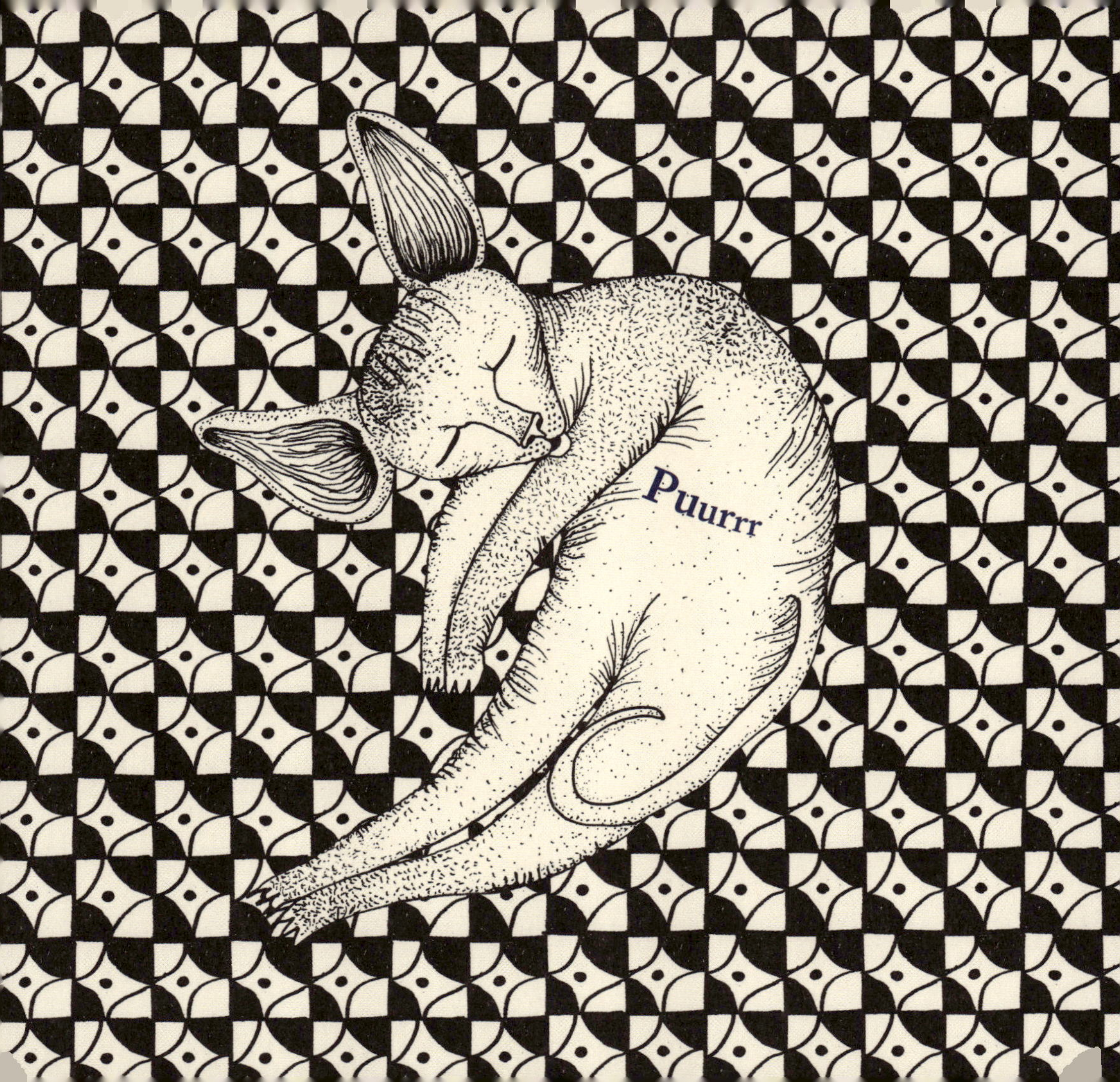
Puurrr

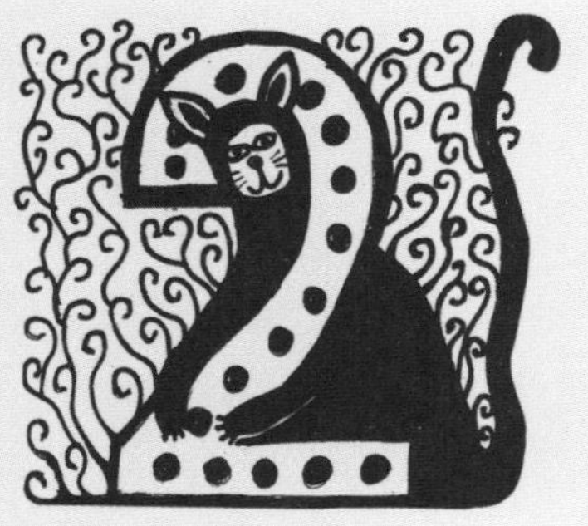

I know you're there...
But it's rude to stare,
Even if I look a tad silly.
But this big, soft settee
Is purrfection for me,
So lying on my tummy
Feels utterly scrummy, you see.

But... I sense you're still lurking,
And possibly still smirking...
Can you please, please just go away!

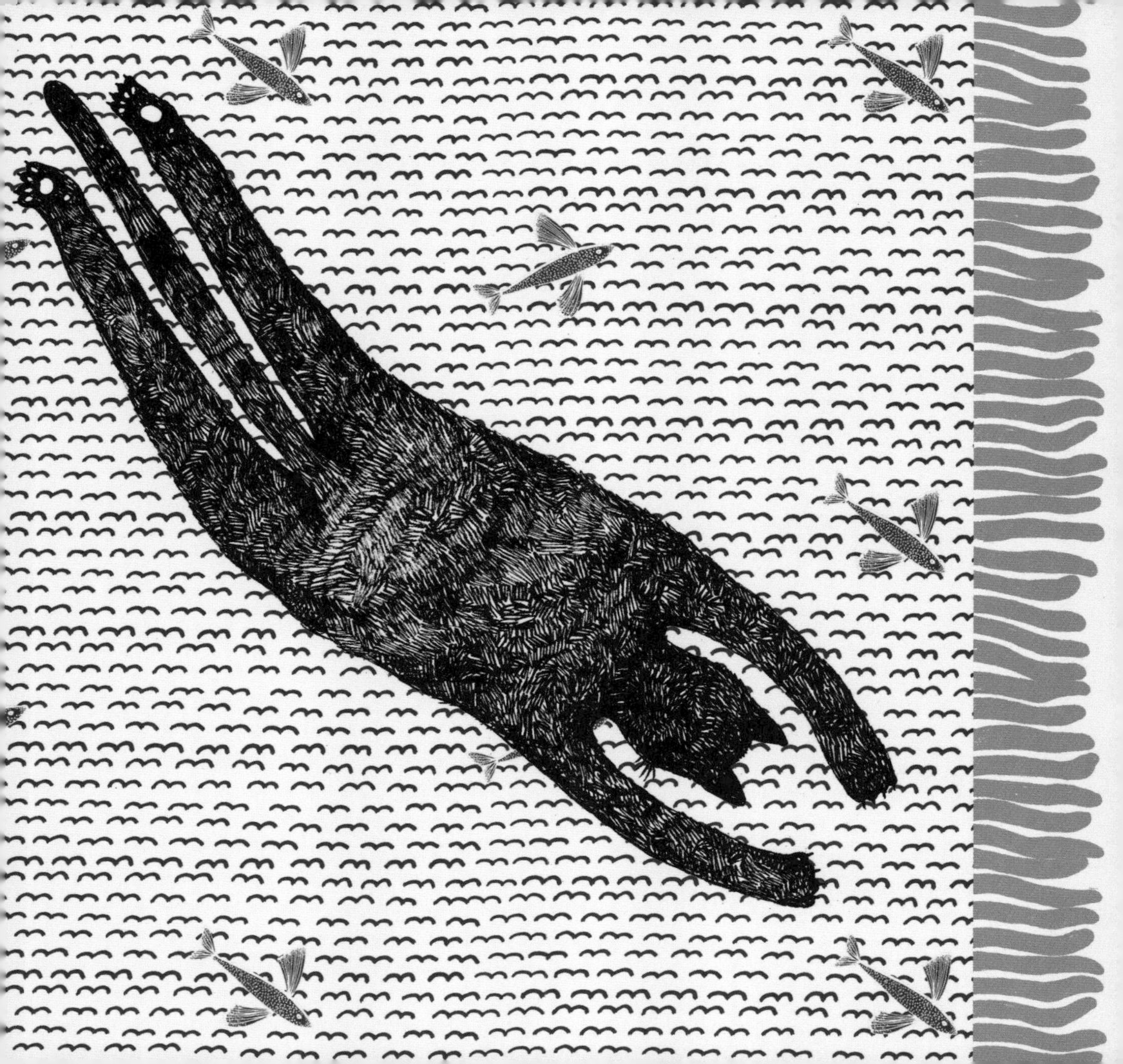

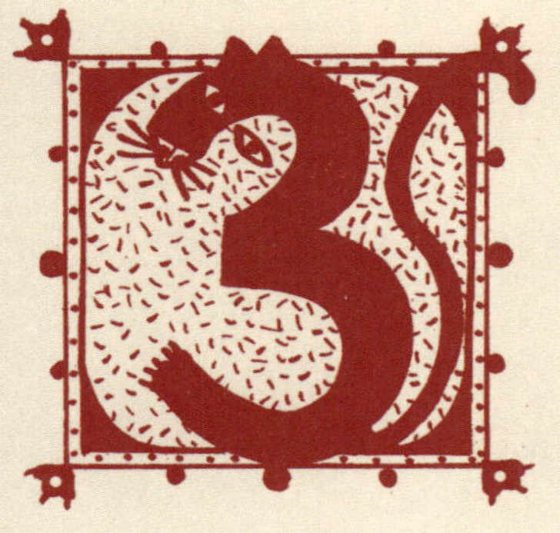

I'm such a hunk, you must admit.
Is any cat more handsome?
My foxy tail is quite a hit –
'An aristocat?' ask some.

I really should have a four-poster bed.
What have I got?
A rotten old blanket instead!

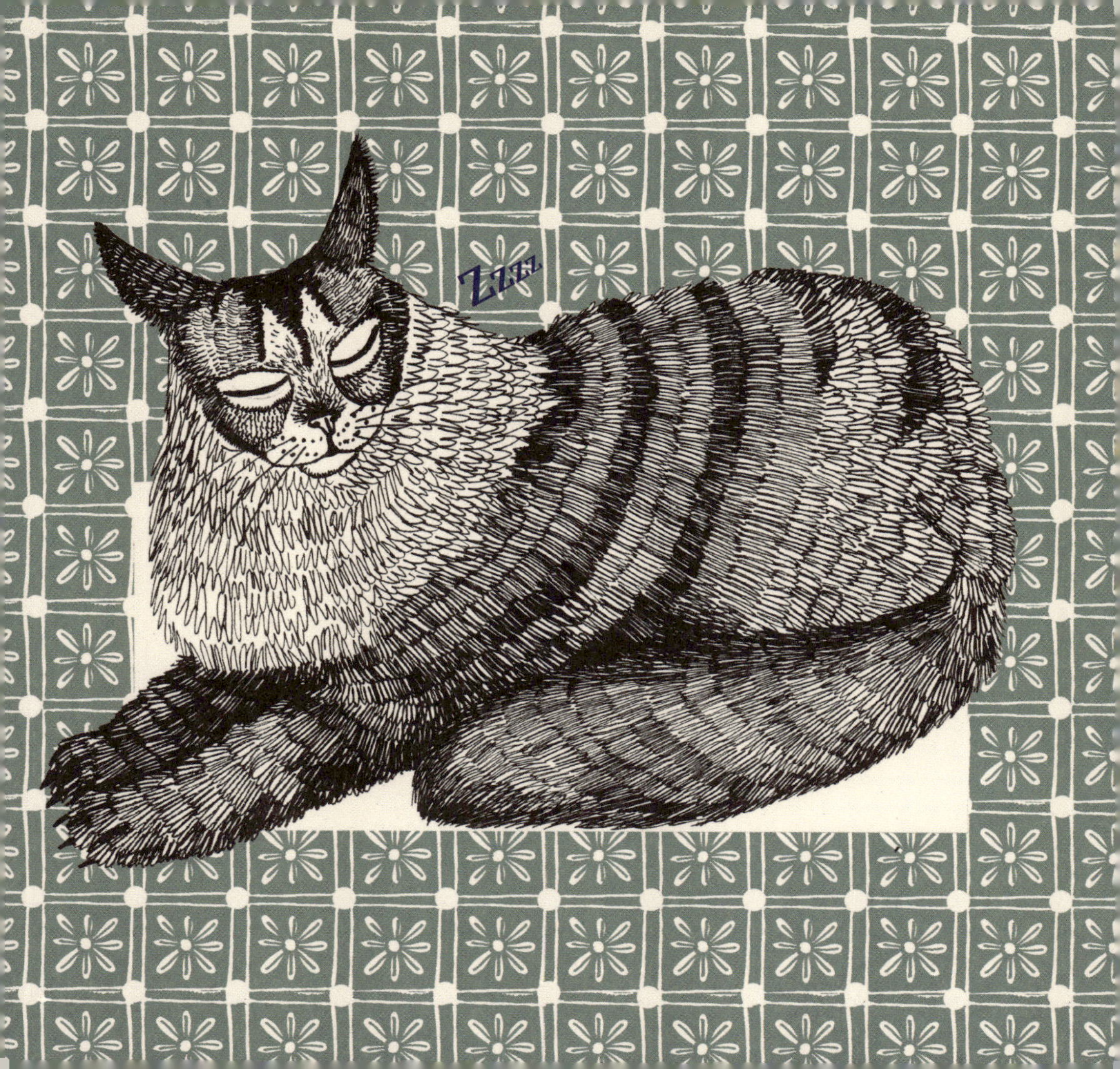
Zzzz

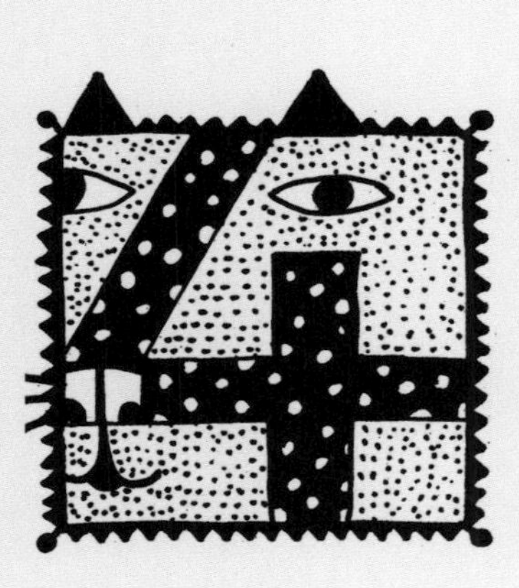

It may look odd...
But rest assured,
This way suits me best.
My legs and tail are quite secure,
Tucked up safely, I guess.

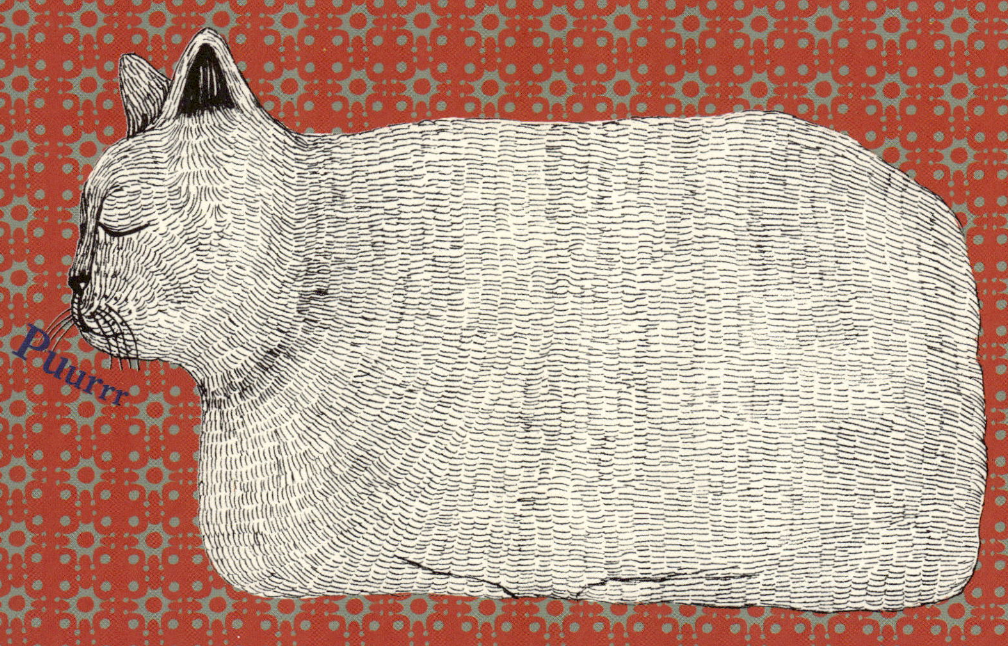
Puurr

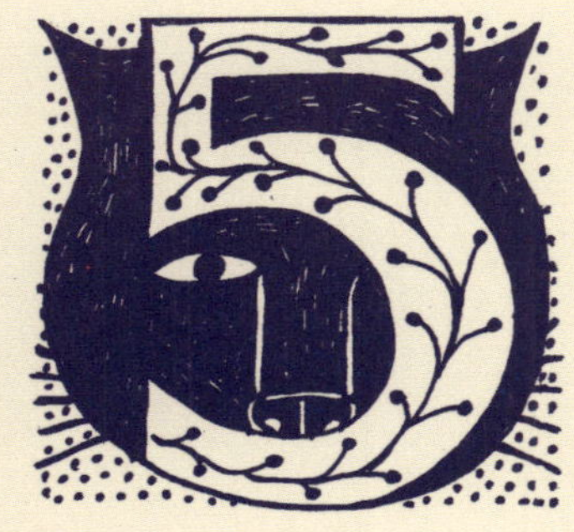

I'm known for my stripes,
And yes, you've guessed…
I'm called Tiger!
A love of napping we share,
But similarities end there.
Jungle life's too hairy,
I'm really quite wary…
I rarely step out of my garden,
I find life quite scary.

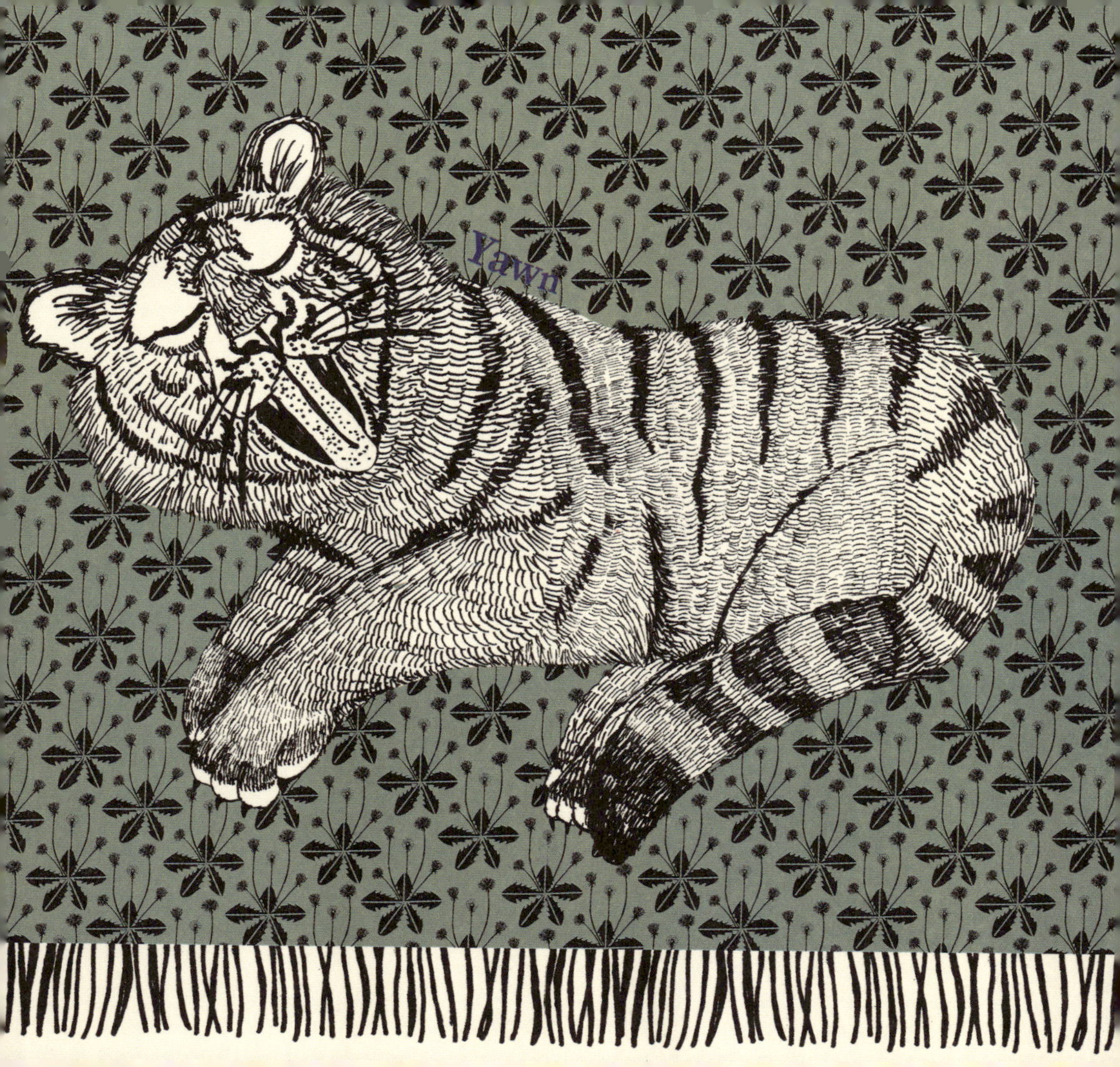
Yawn

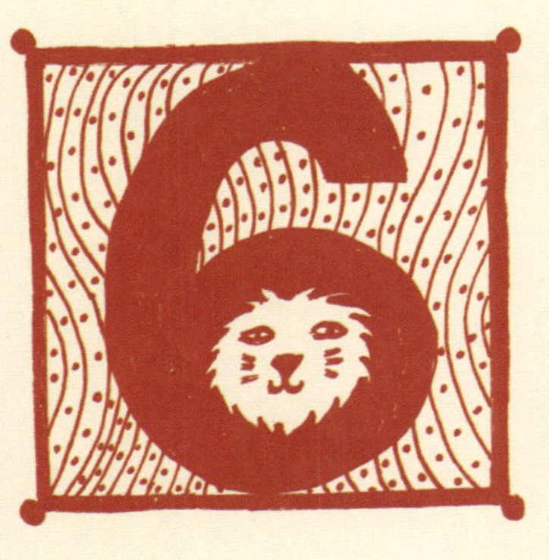

Keep-fit cat is dreaming
Of skipping to and fro.
Even while she's sleeping,
She tries to touch her toes!

She goes through all her paces,
Even dreams of winning races!

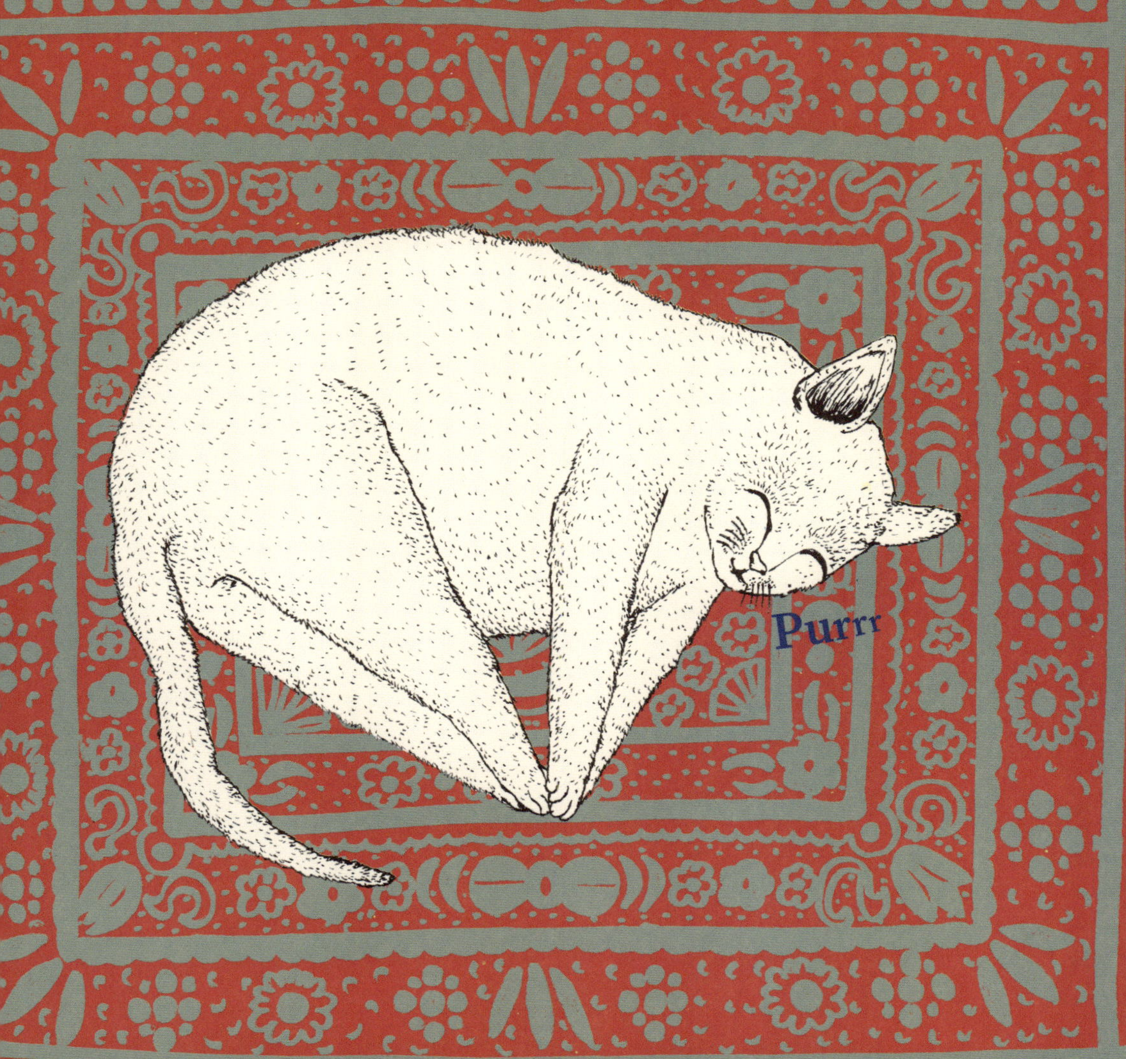
Purrr

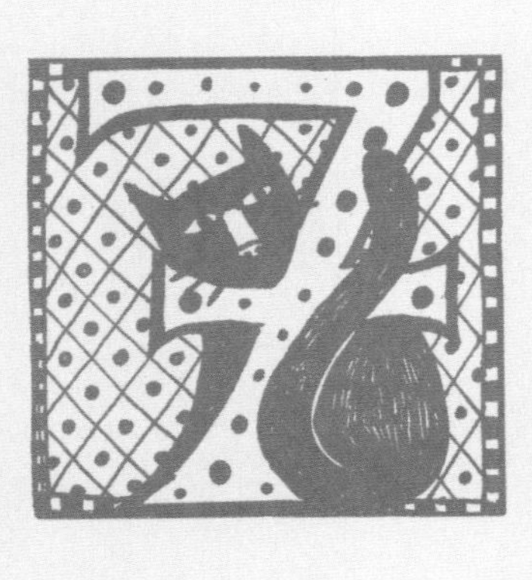

I like to shimmy on my back,
To find the perfect spot.
It's not as easy as it sounds –
A skill that can't be taught!

North, south, east or west,
Until I find the place that's best.

Oooooh... found it!

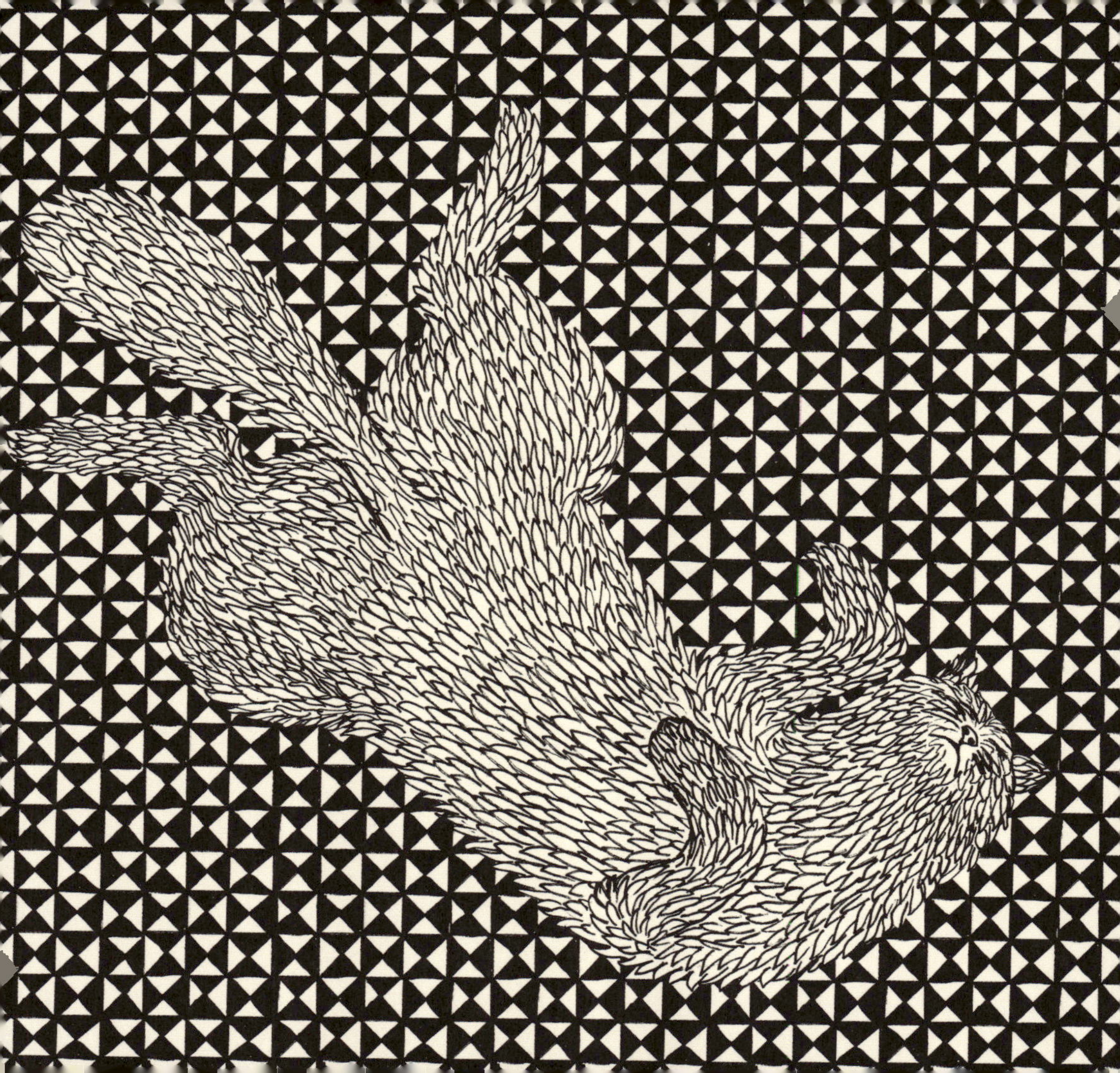

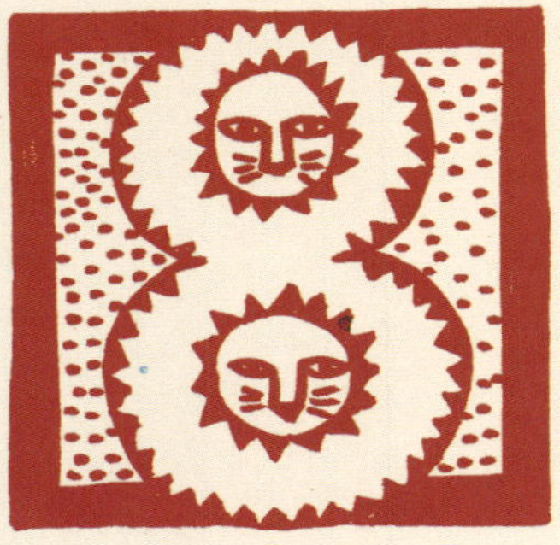

Trying to sleep like my owner,
As this way suits him fine.
I don't mean to be a moaner...
But this really needs to be refined.
Perhaps it's time he took advice?
From a cat like me – to be precise!

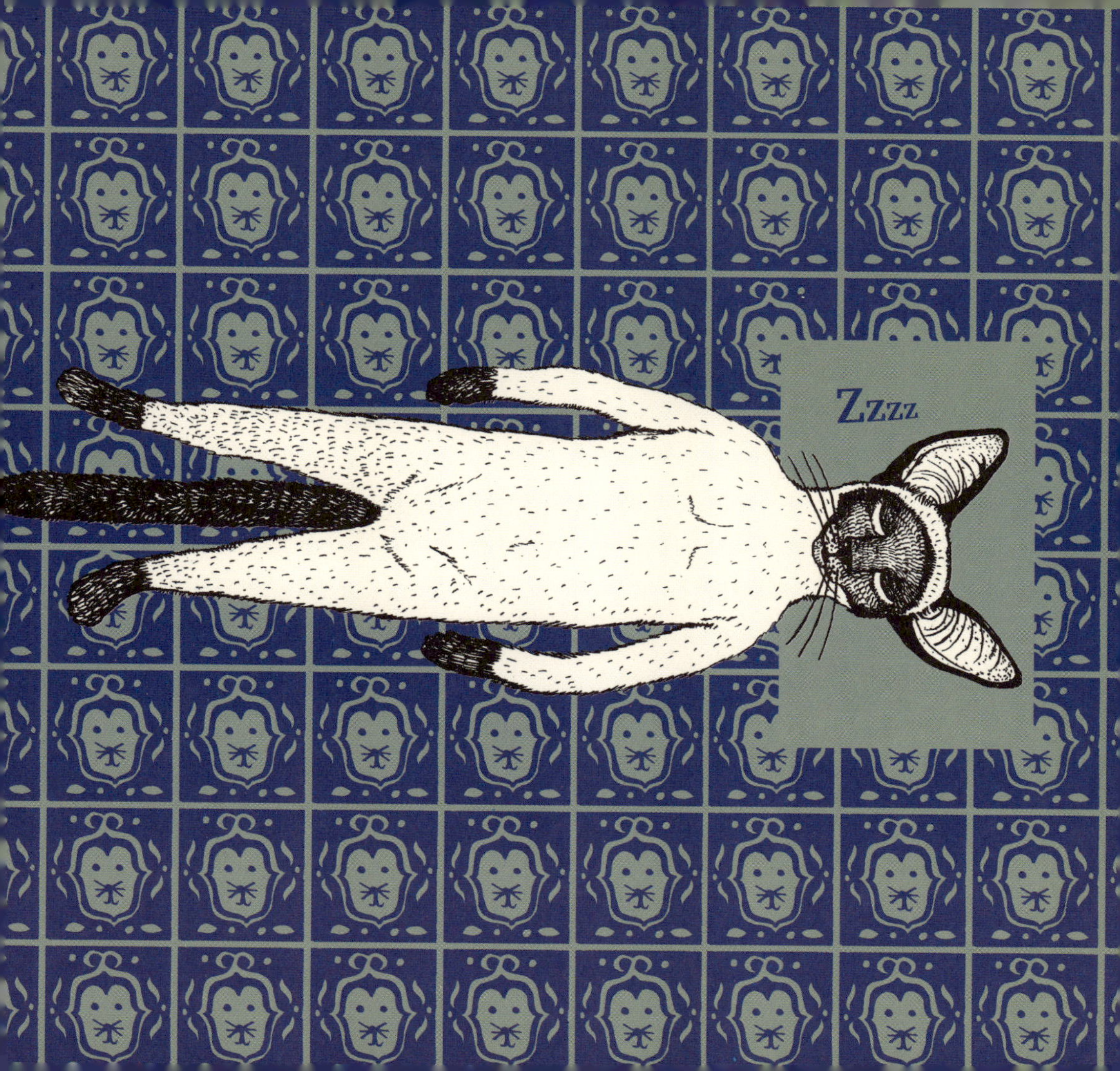
Zzzz

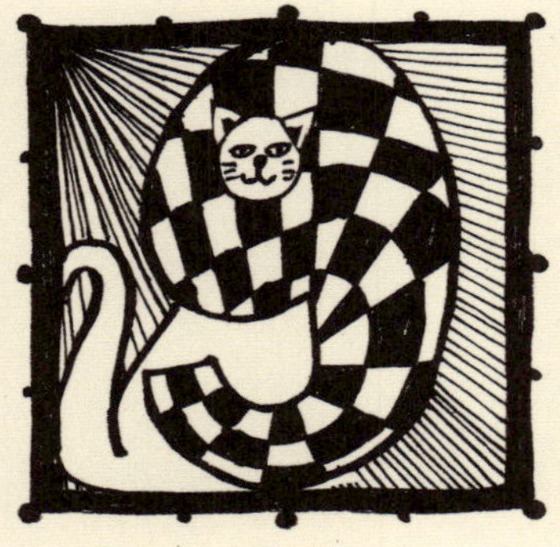

This may look rather boring –
A cat with little flair?
But she's fast asleep and snoring
So it's none of your affair!
She could try other poses
But this way suits her best,
So go away and leave her
To get on with her rest!

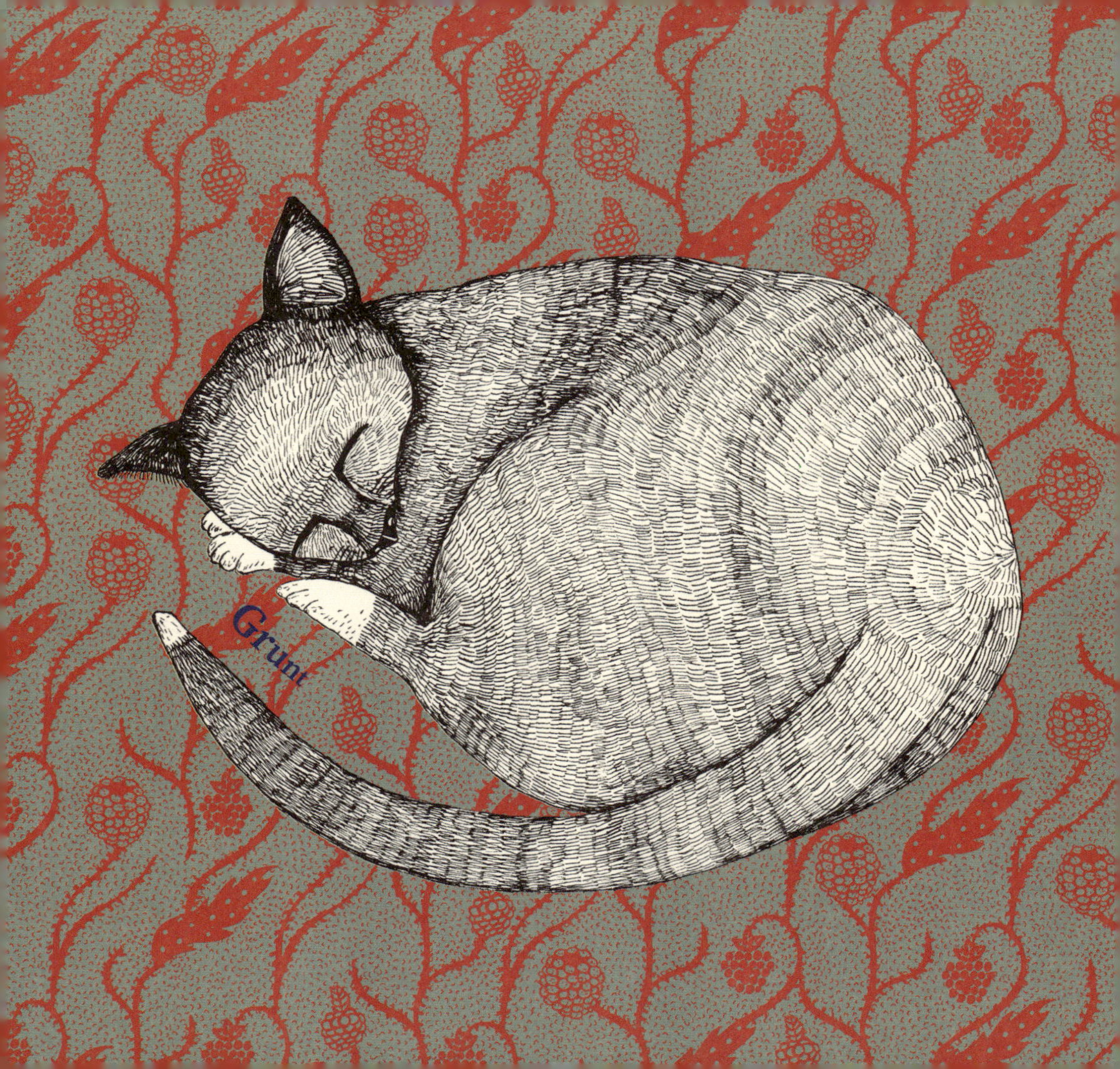
Grunt

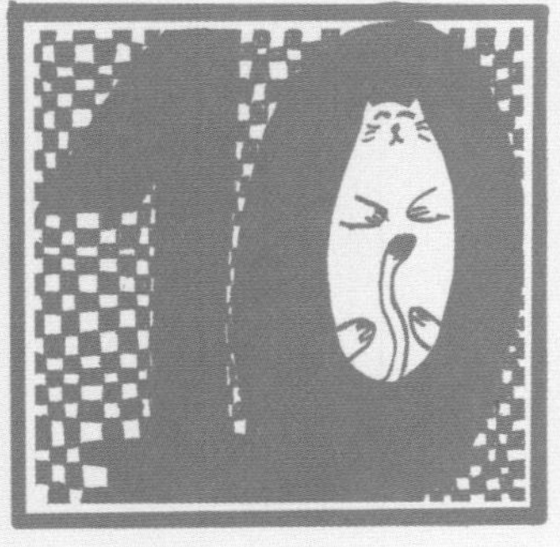

My food bowl has shrunk,
Tinned food tastes like junk,
And a big, hairy dog
Makes my life such a slog!

But I'll have a quick snooze
To forget all my blues.
Lose myself in a dream
Of a big bowl of cream!

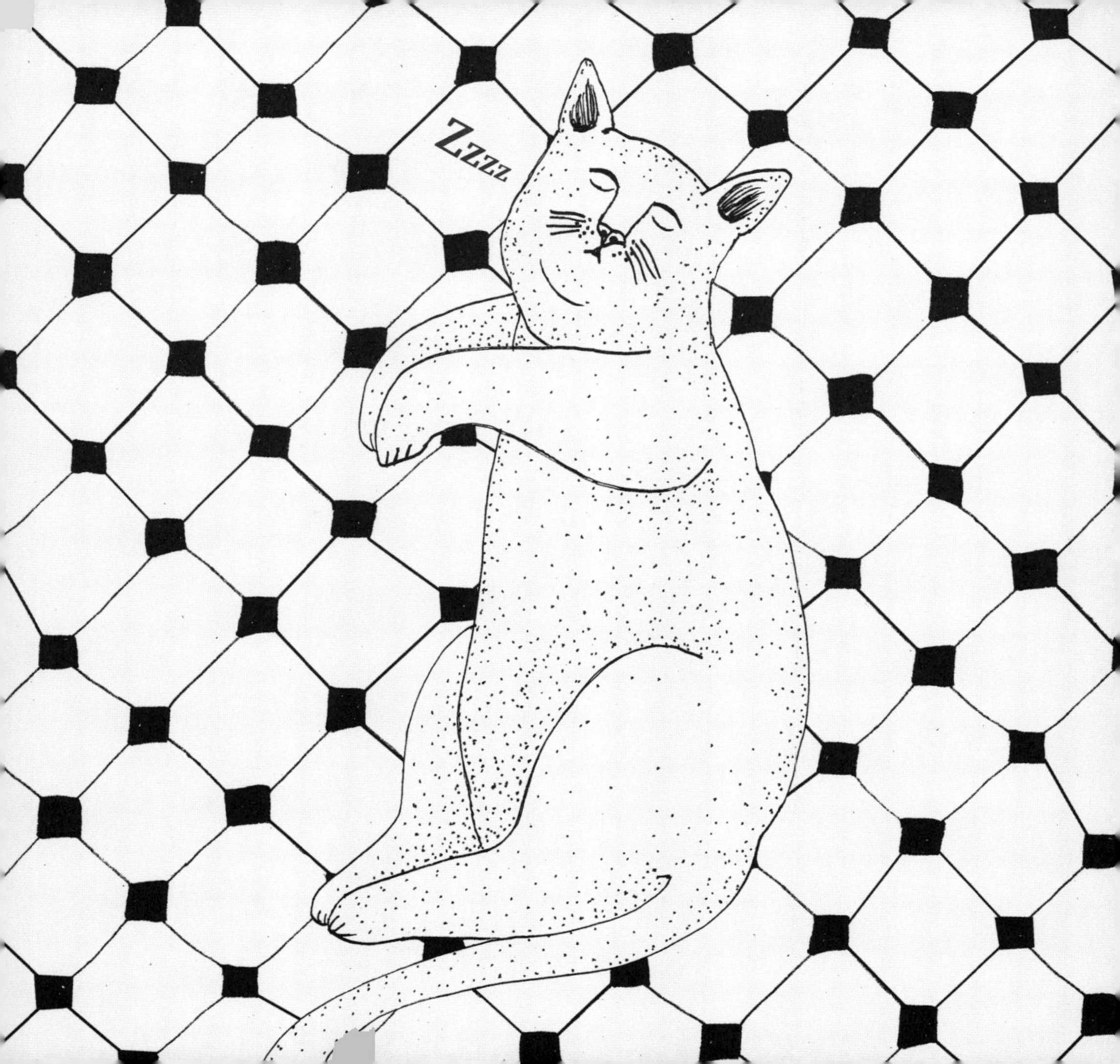
Zzzz

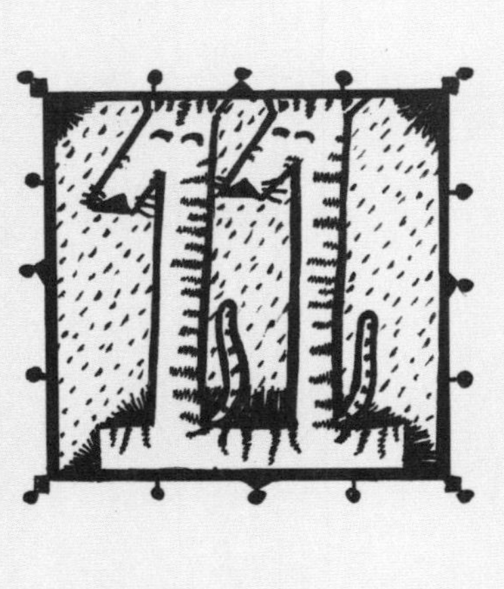

Back to front
And upside down,
My cat is simply
The wrong way round!
His sense of direction
Is really confusing.
I suppose he's comfy?
It's... quite amusing.

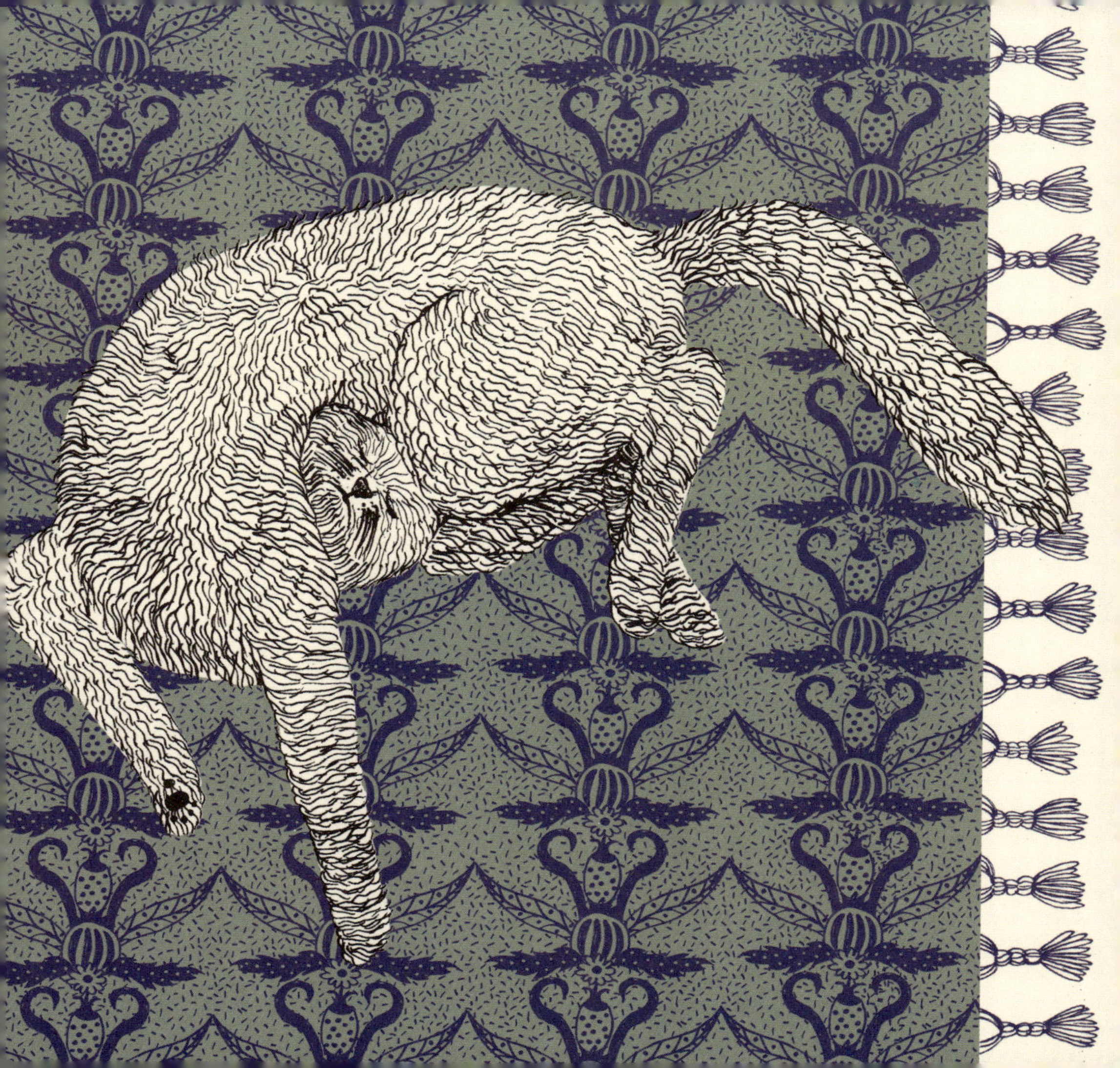

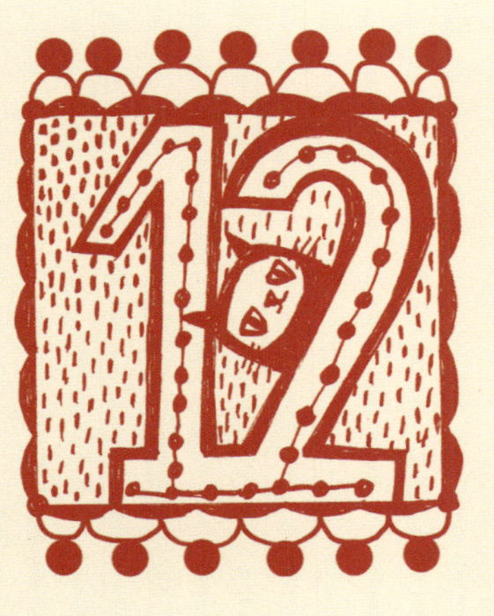

This way, that way,
Left a bit, right a bit,
Legs up, legs out.
Comfort? You've guessed...
I'm still working it out!

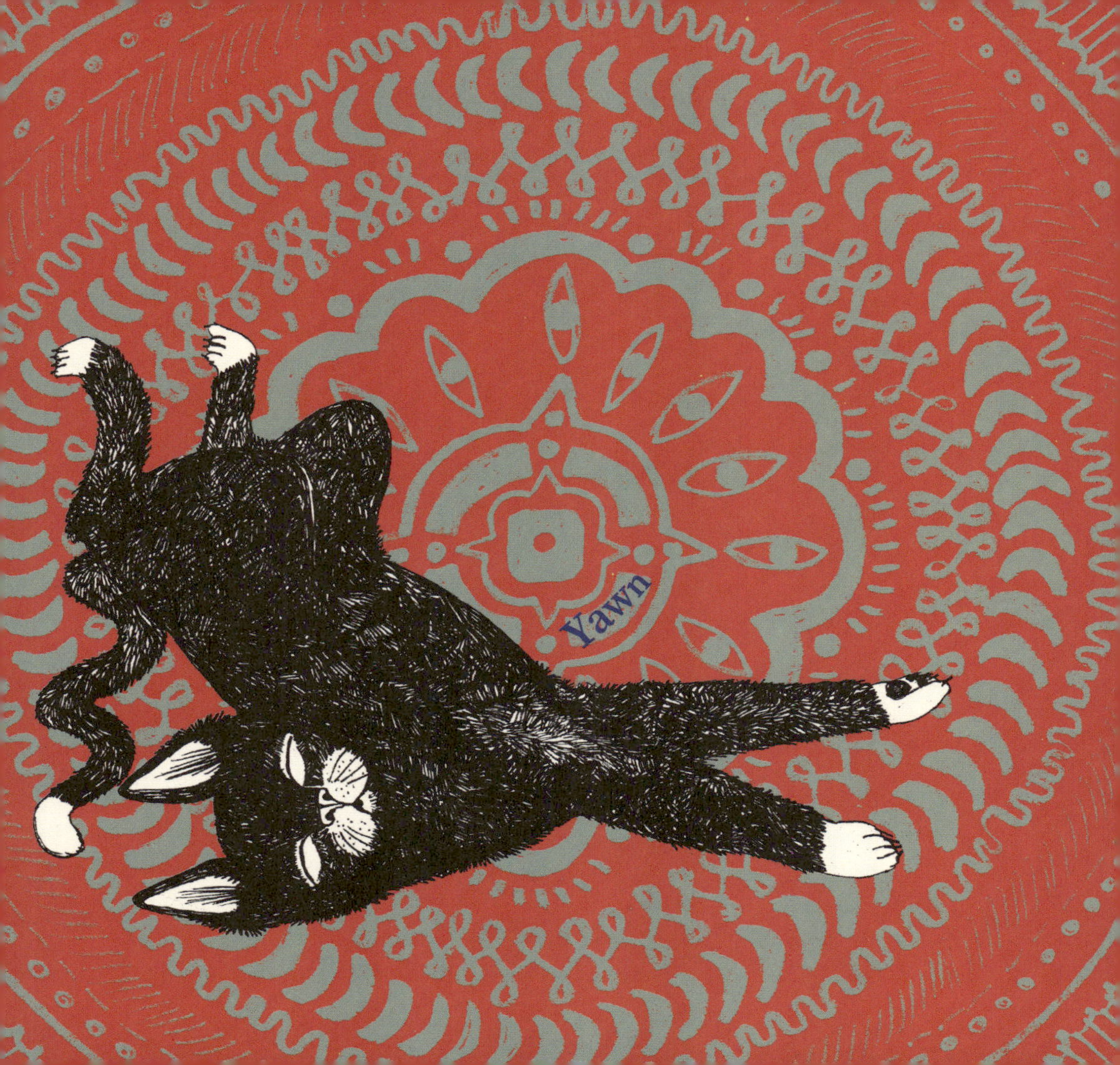
Yawn

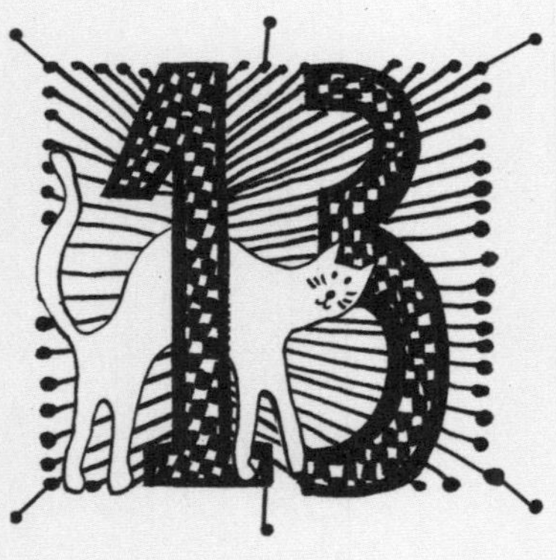

At least once in your life
Roll up in a ball and...
Squeeze yourself into a box.
It may feel rather square,
But what do you care?
It's as snug as a pair of socks.

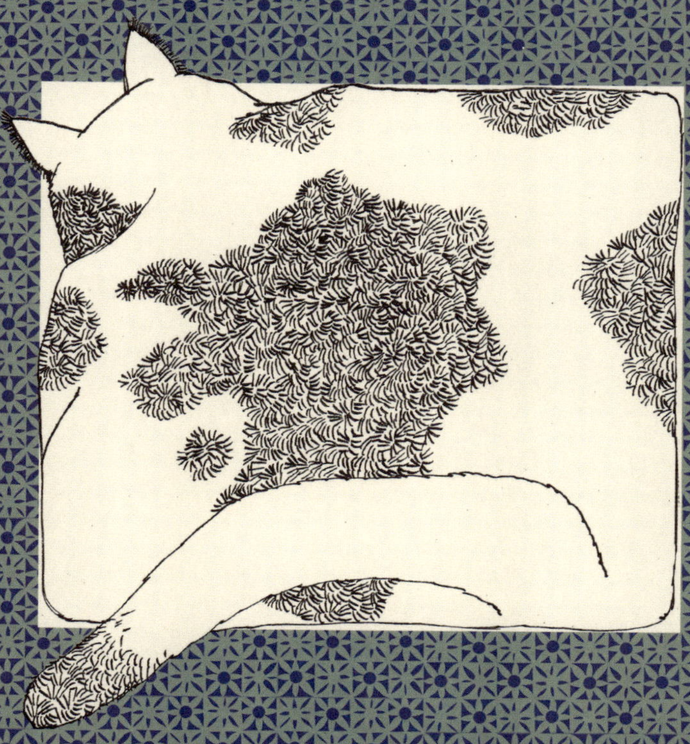

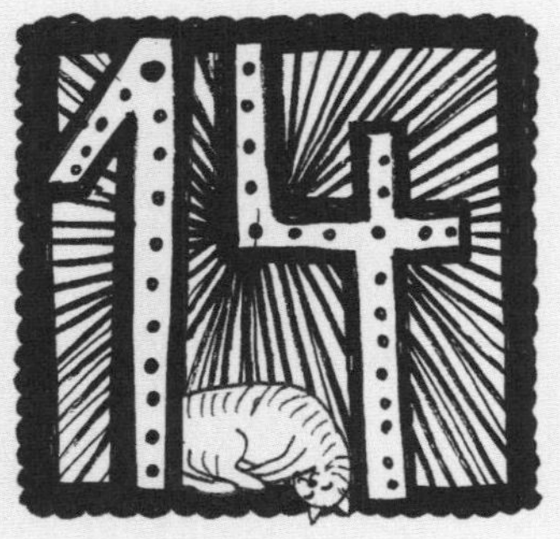

It's jolly hard to have a good nap,
Where nobody else can see me.
Other cats manage to sleep in peace
But my spots always reveal me.
If only I was an everyday moggie,
Instead of one with breeding?

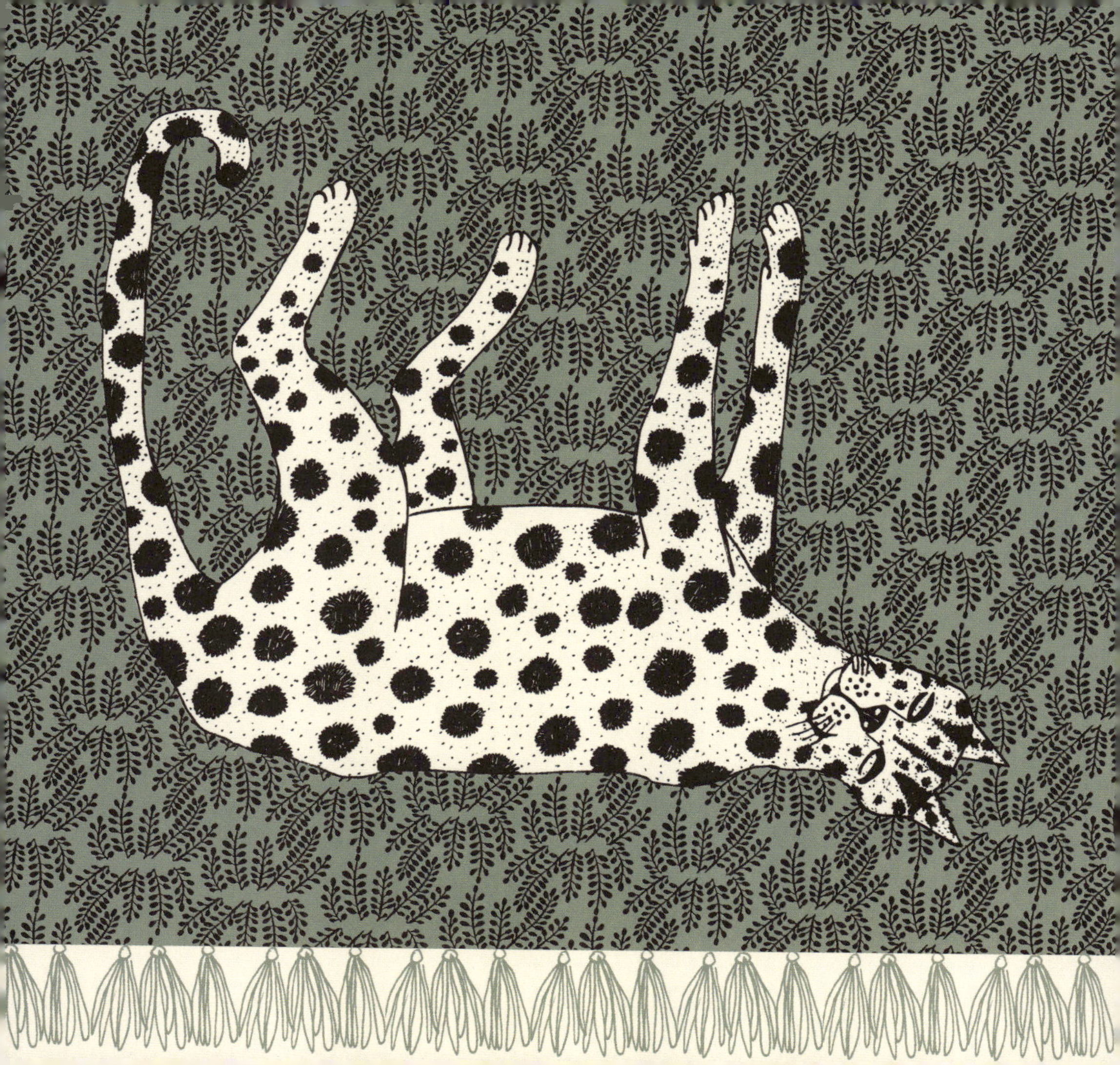

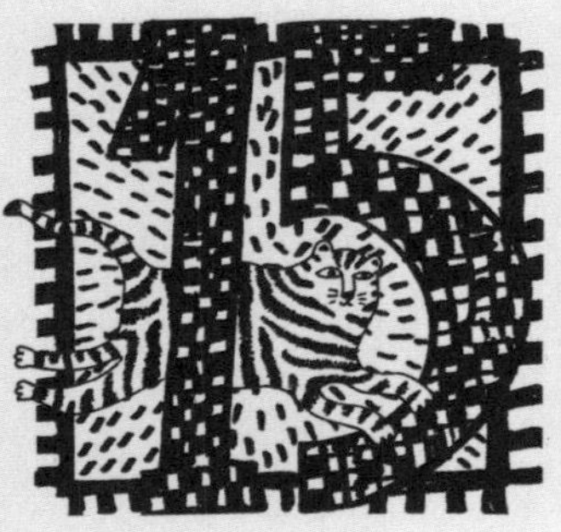

This is not cat lethargy,
It's a cat saving energy.
It's an art he's perfected –
With no doubt or mistake,
He's sure to be asleep
More than he's ever awake!

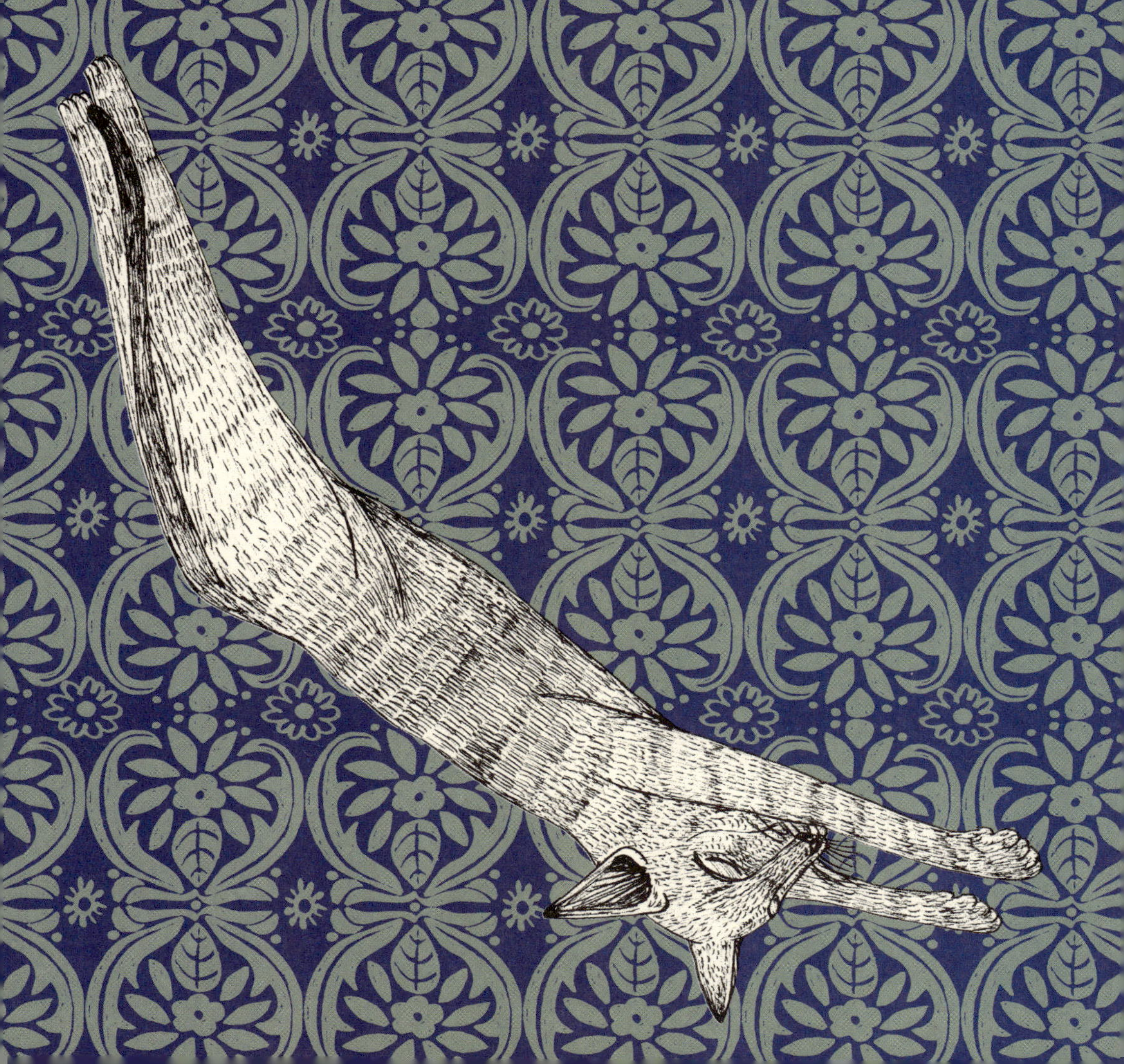

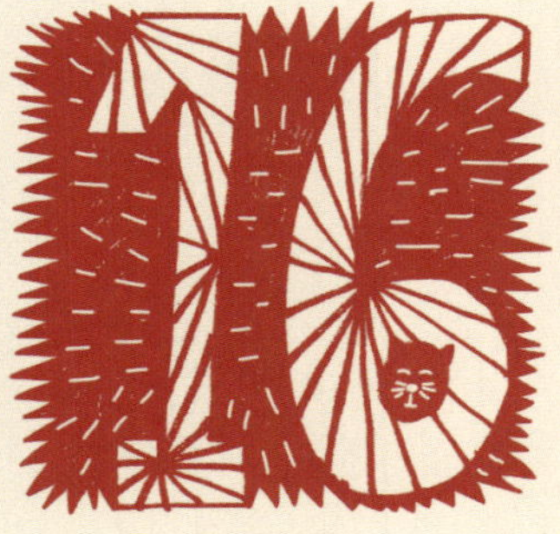

Short of a pillow?
Think out of the box...
It's time to lie low
With a convenient hot dog!

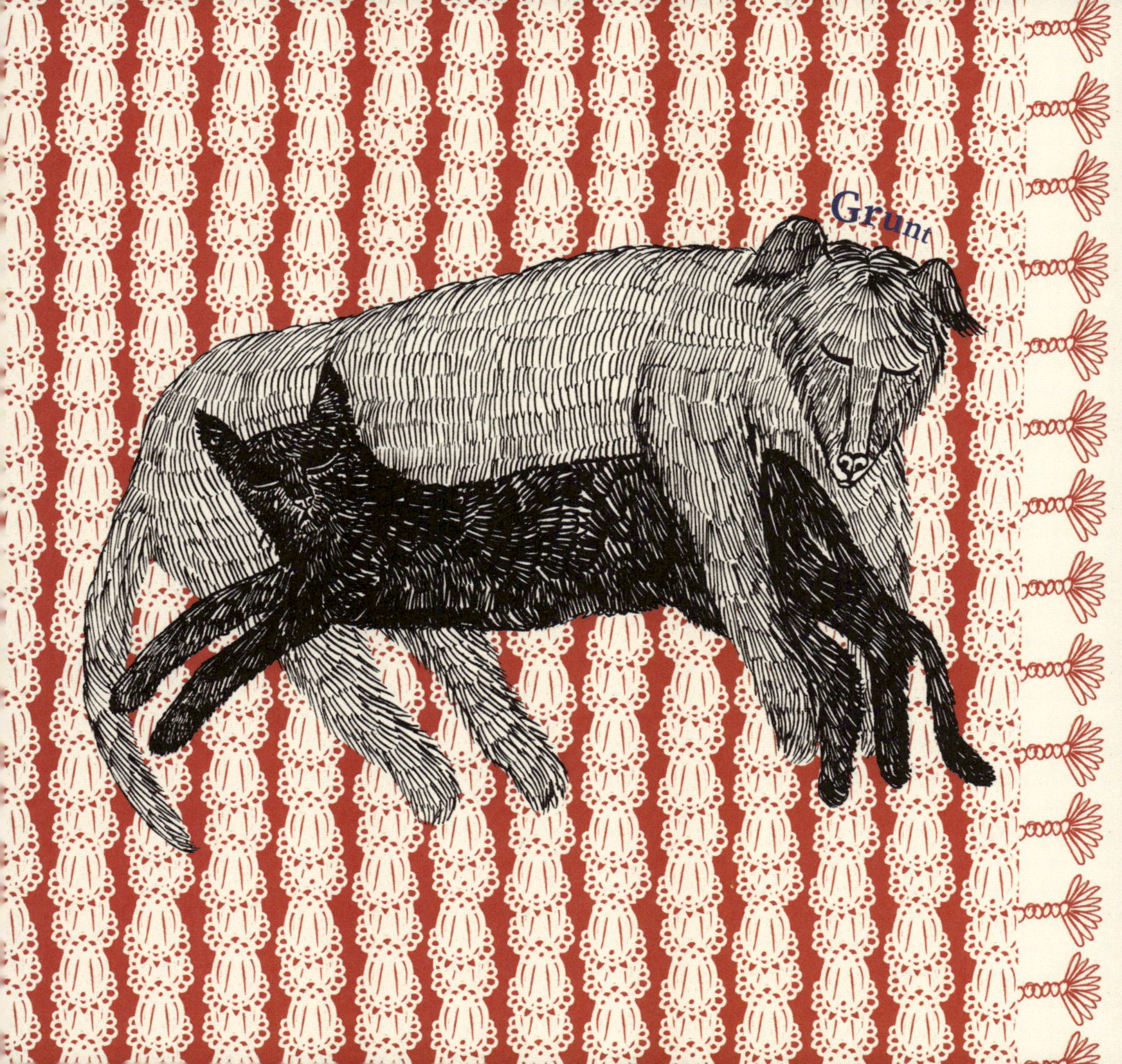
Grunt

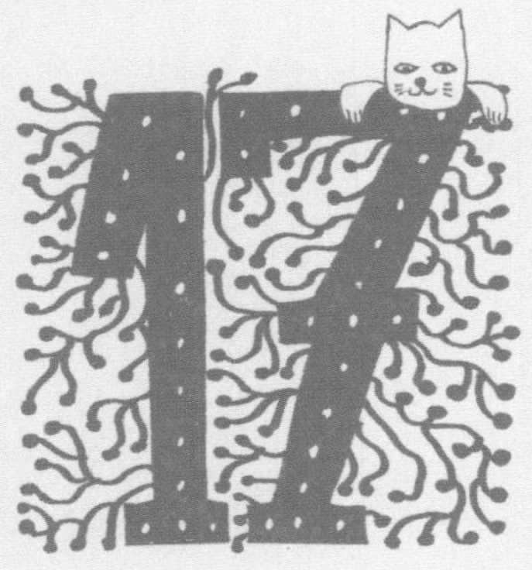

My bowl is still empty,
There's no milk to drink,
May as well just roll over,
For another forty winks.

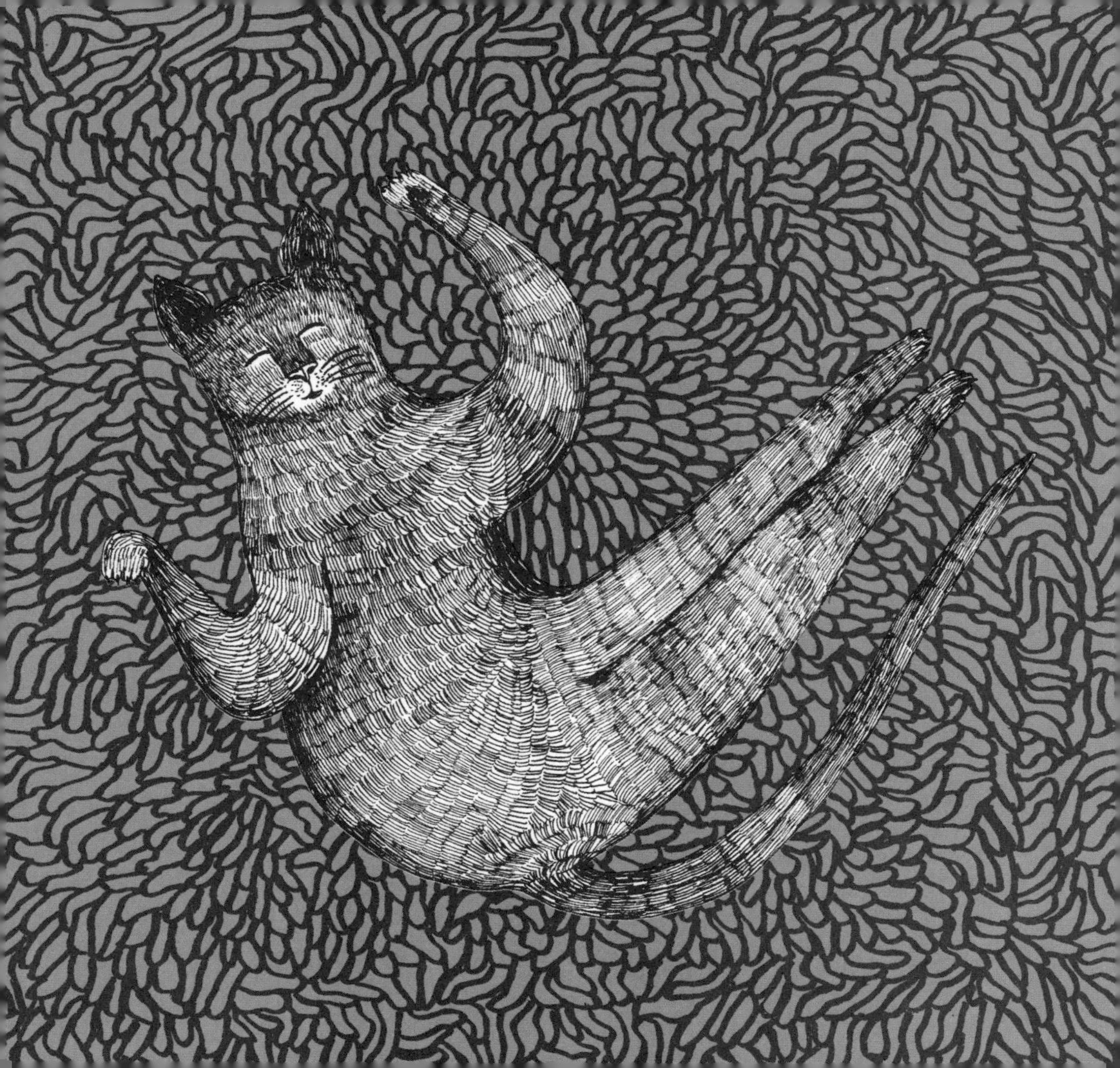

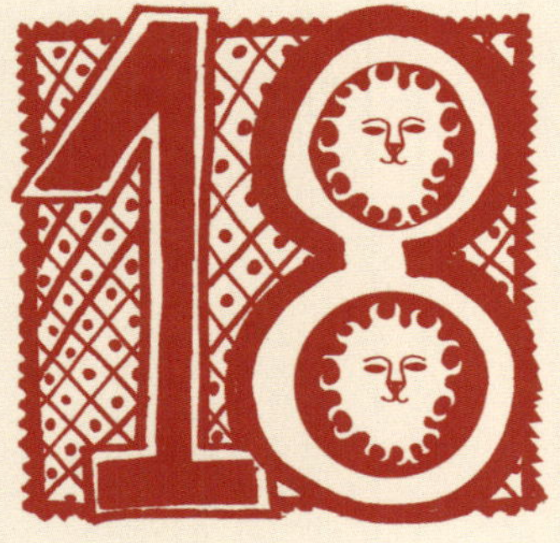

I like sleeping out on the garden wall,
But I've grown too big…
Or the catflap's too small.
If no one's at home to open the door,
I'm happy to sleep on the kitchen floor.

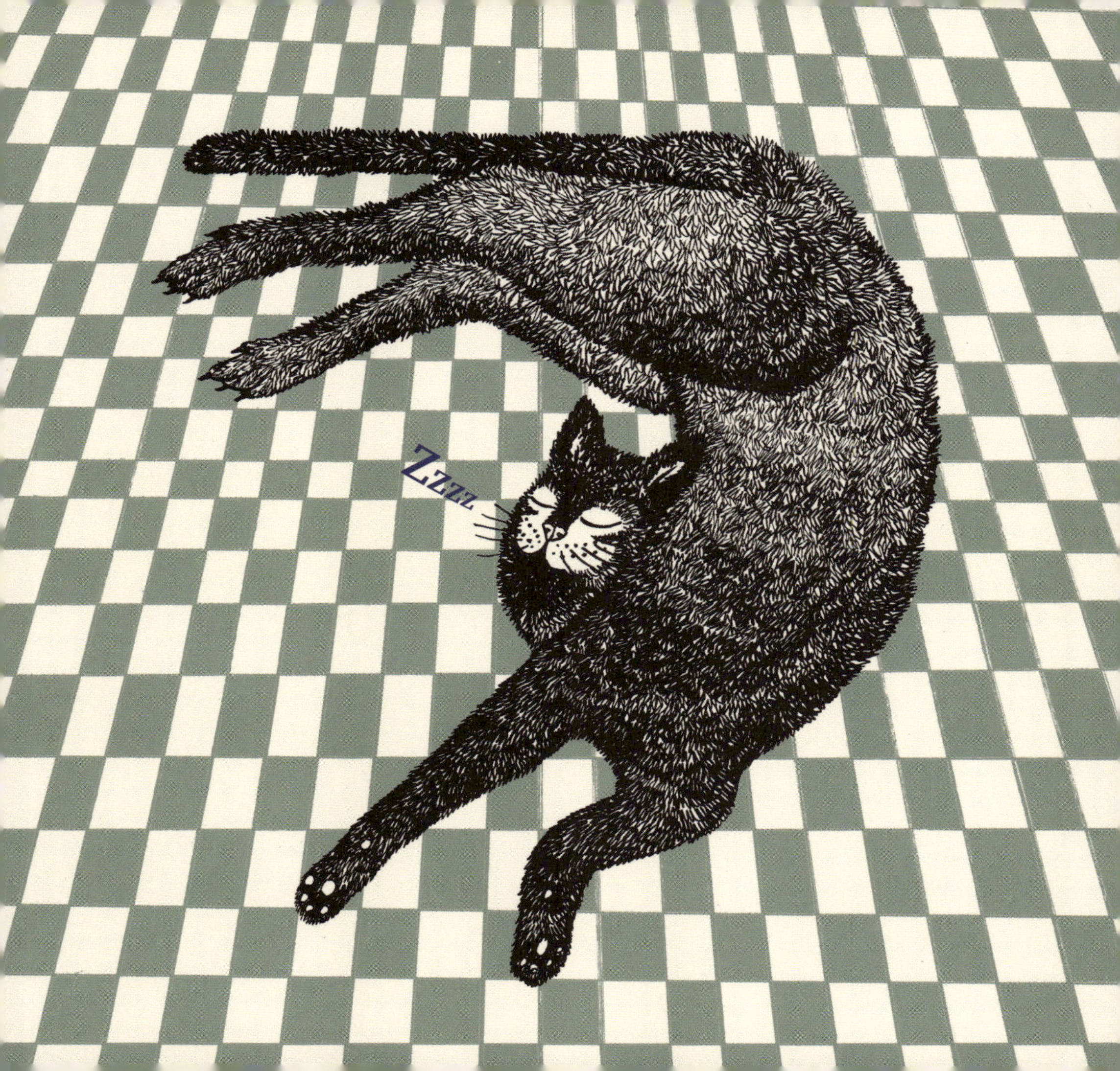

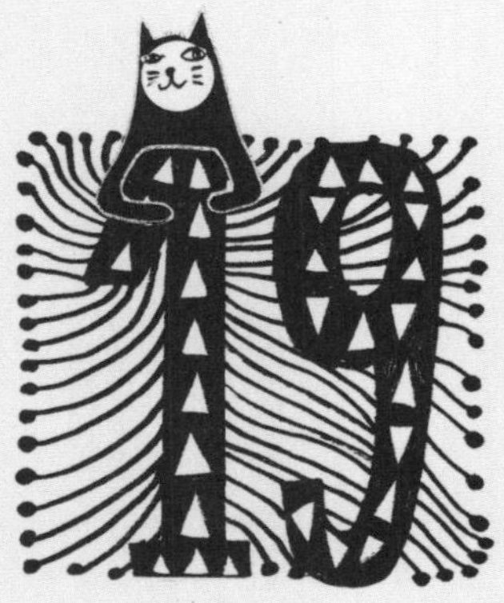

Why sleep alone, in your room,
If there's a mate with whom to spoon?
A twosome,
A threesome,
Or four or more
Will soon provide you
With warmth galore!

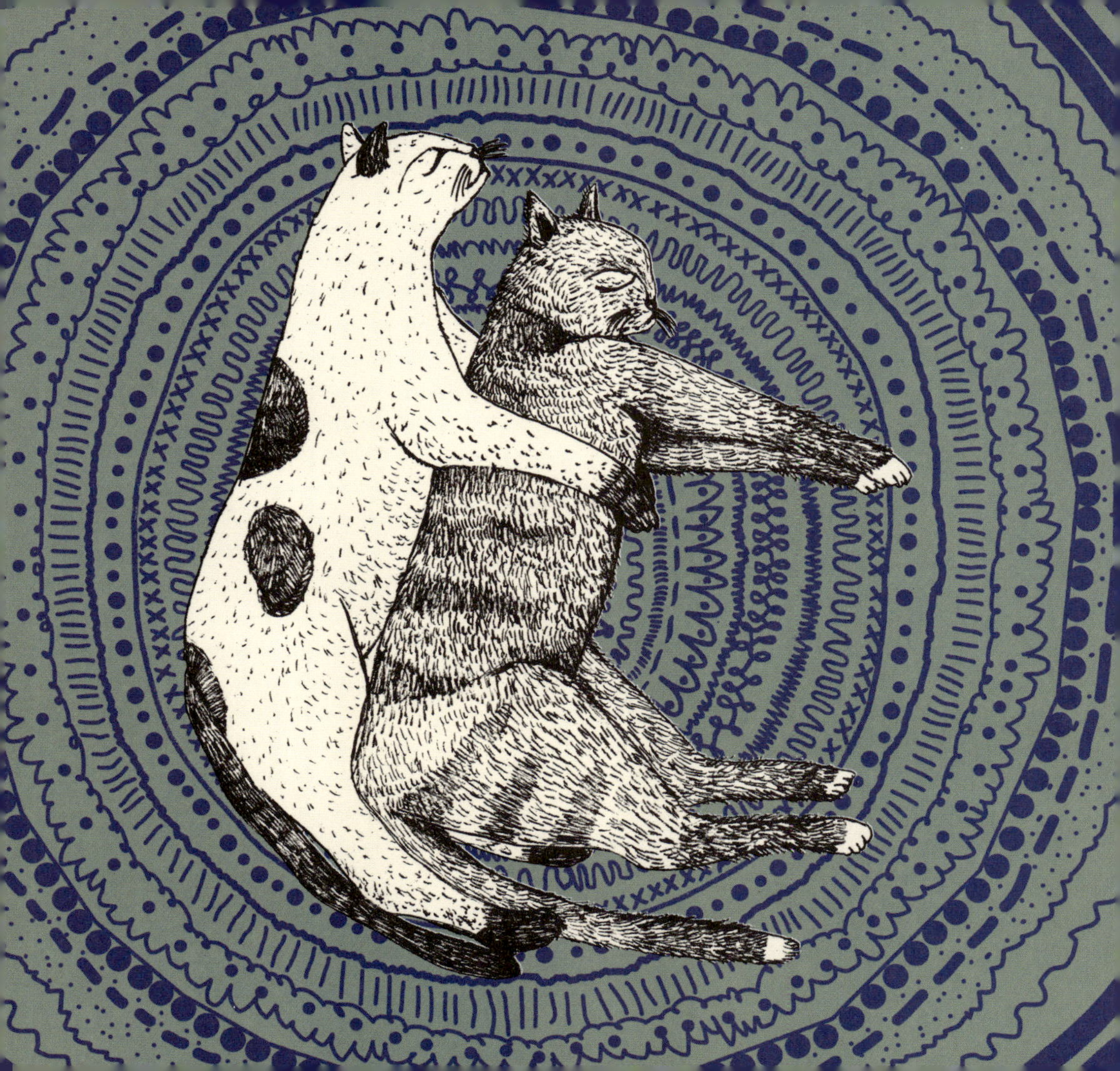

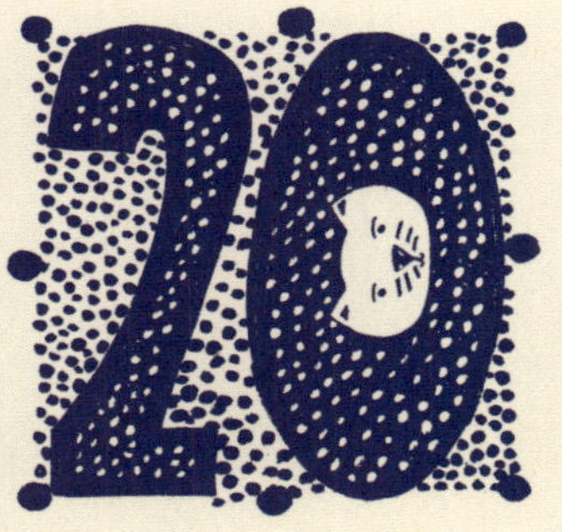

Lived for longer than I care to recall,
And I've slept in all possible ways.
The time has come to 'think off the wall'
And find a new pose for today.
This one certainly is quite a change,
But I have to say... it feels mighty strange.

... I think I've invented cat yoga!

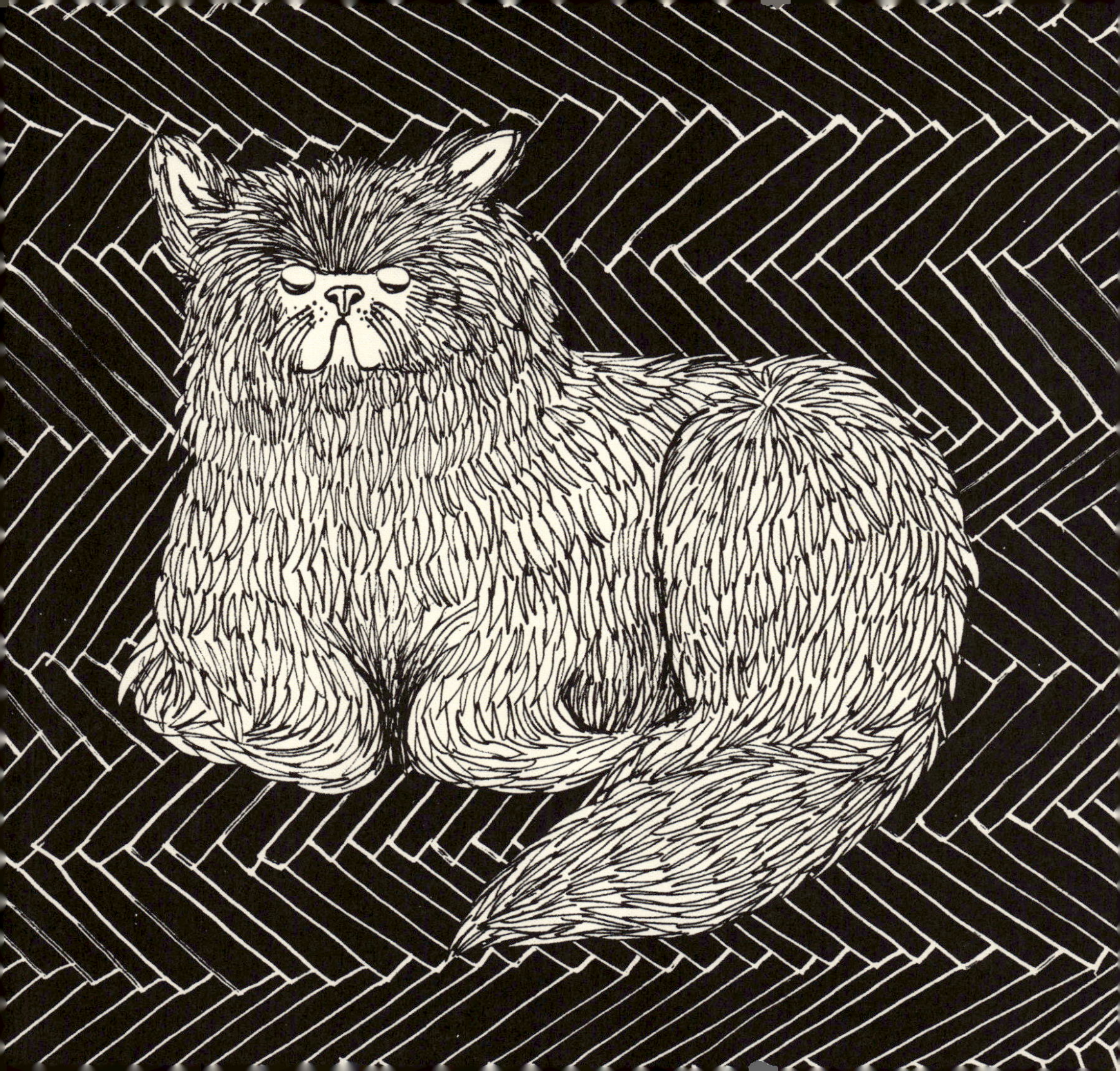

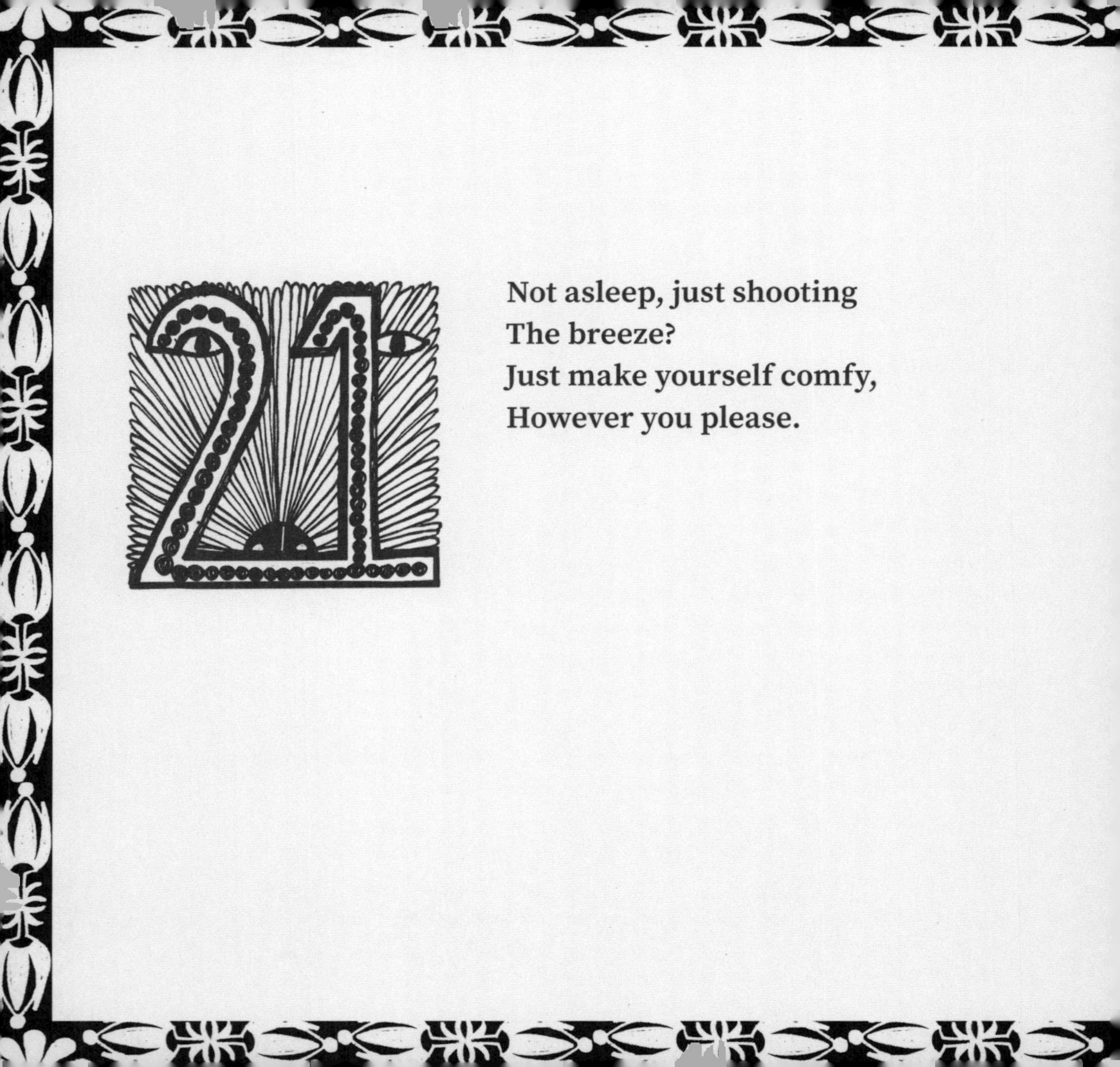

Not asleep, just shooting
The breeze?
Just make yourself comfy,
However you please.

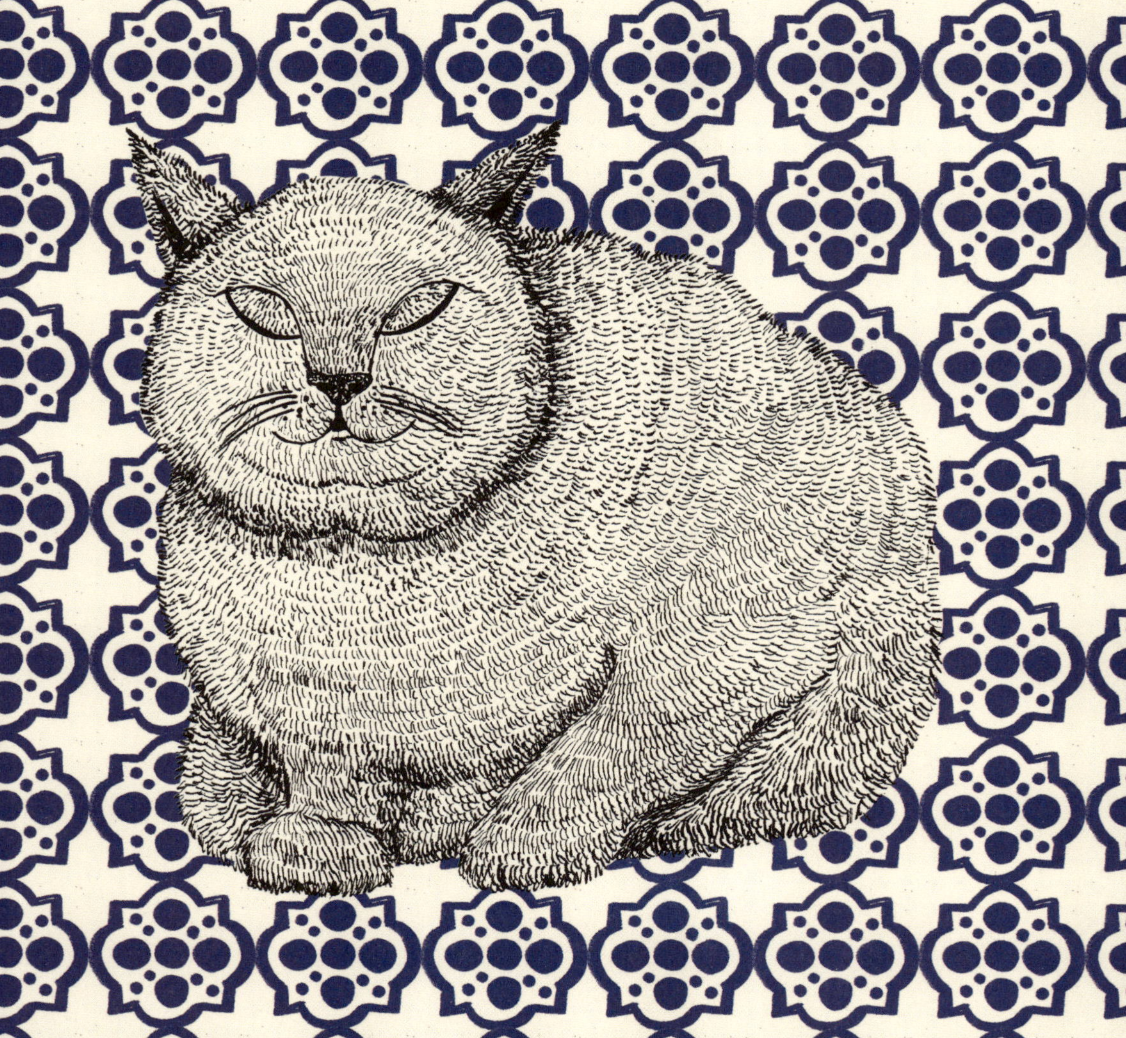

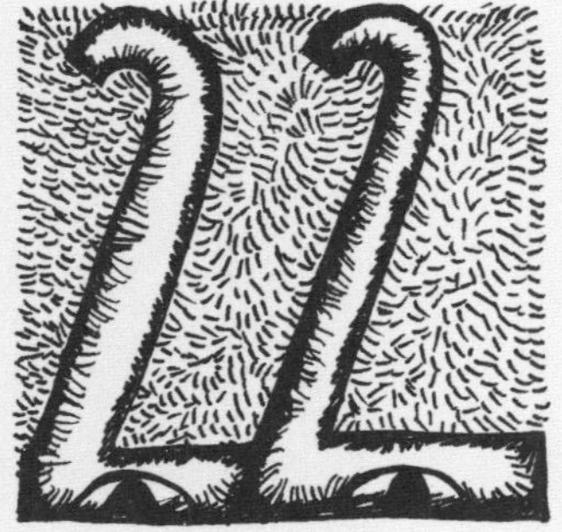

Some cats are simply bone idle,
Some like to hunt and explore.
Those that opt for a quiet life,
Usually park behind the front door!

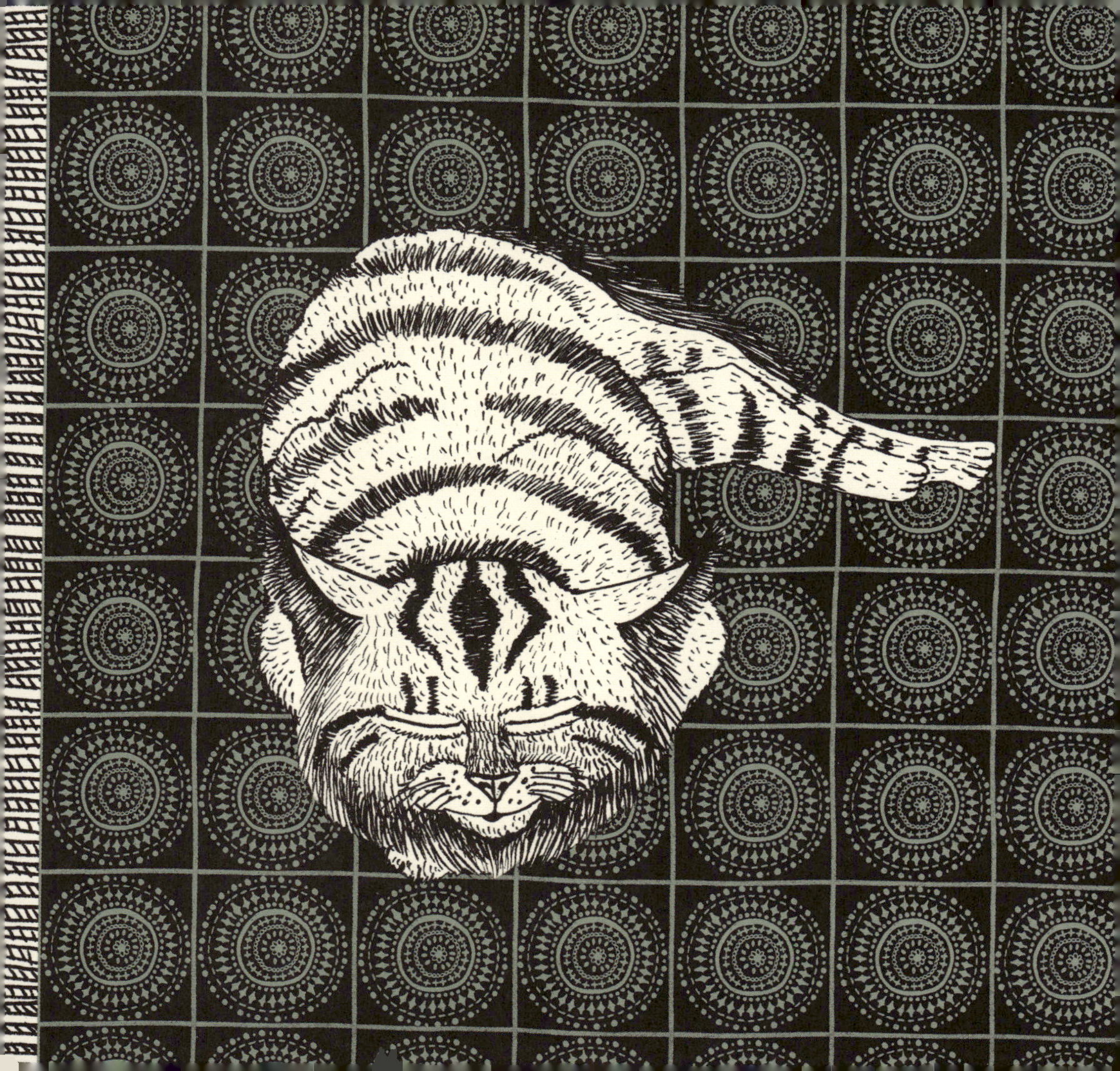

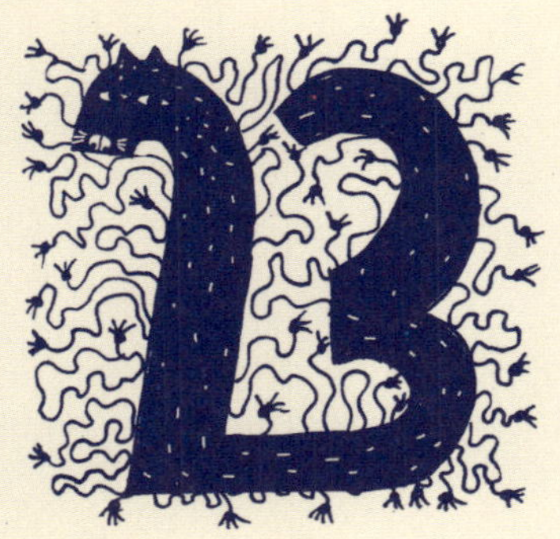

I'm a very old pussycat now,
A 'statesman', you might say.
I'm not so fast on my legs now,
But no signs of turning grey!
Age does bring some benefits now,
It really must be said,
As nobody minds at all now,
If they find me asleep on the bed.

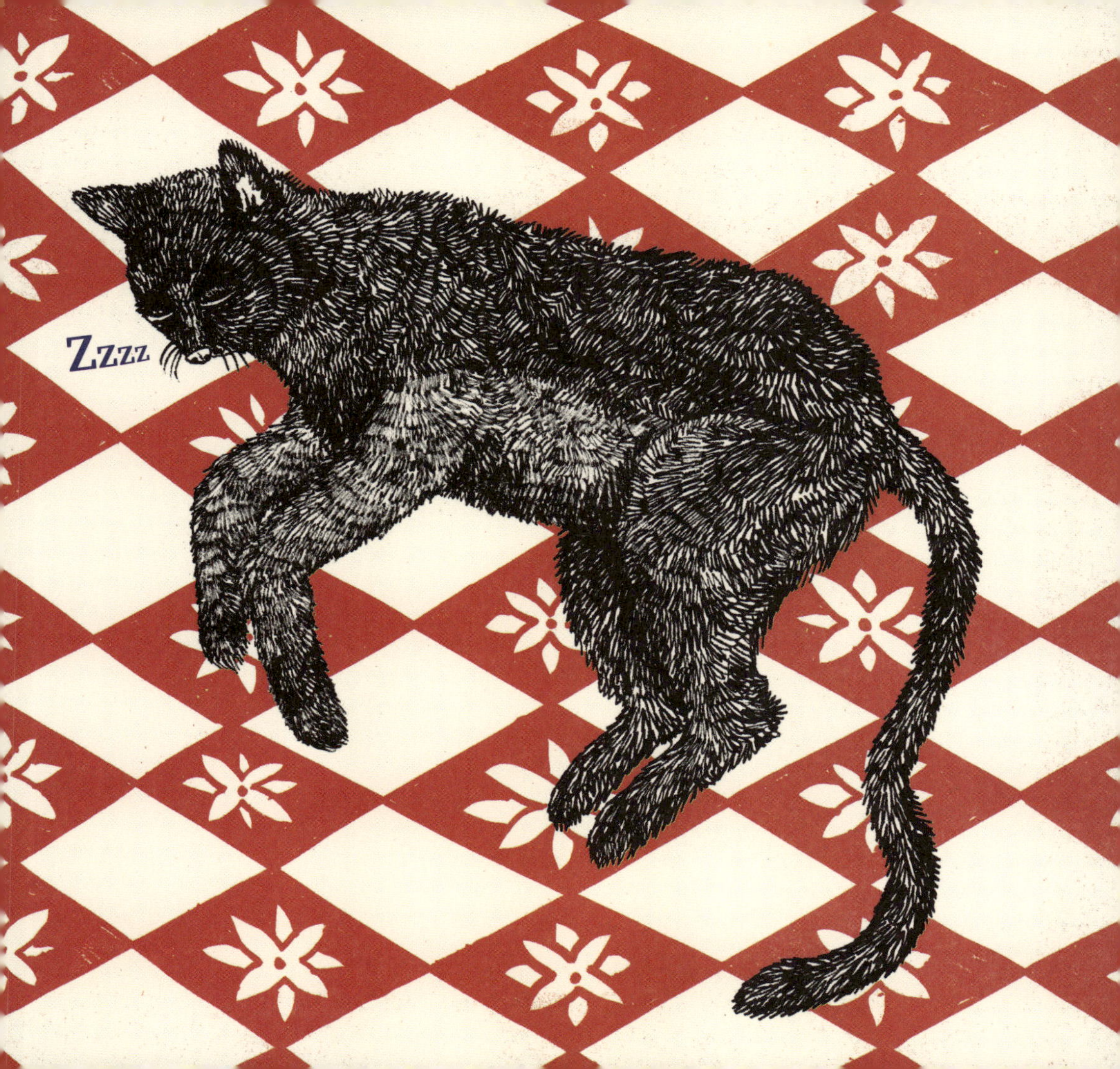

Zzzz

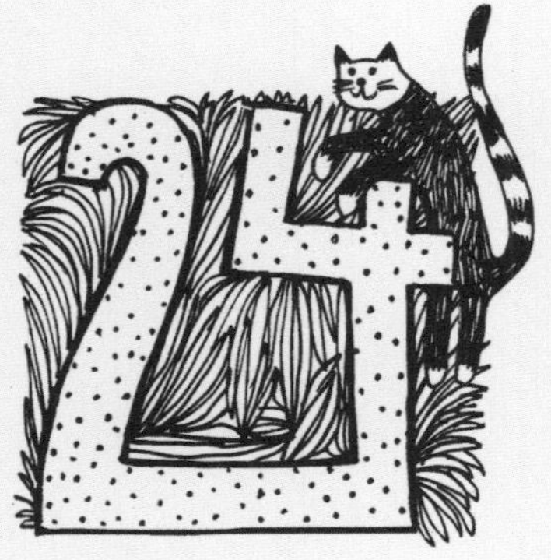

Don't lose out on your zzzzz's,
Because a dog is about –
Snooze with your claws in the air.
Then even the silliest dog can work out
That this cat means business... 'Beware!'

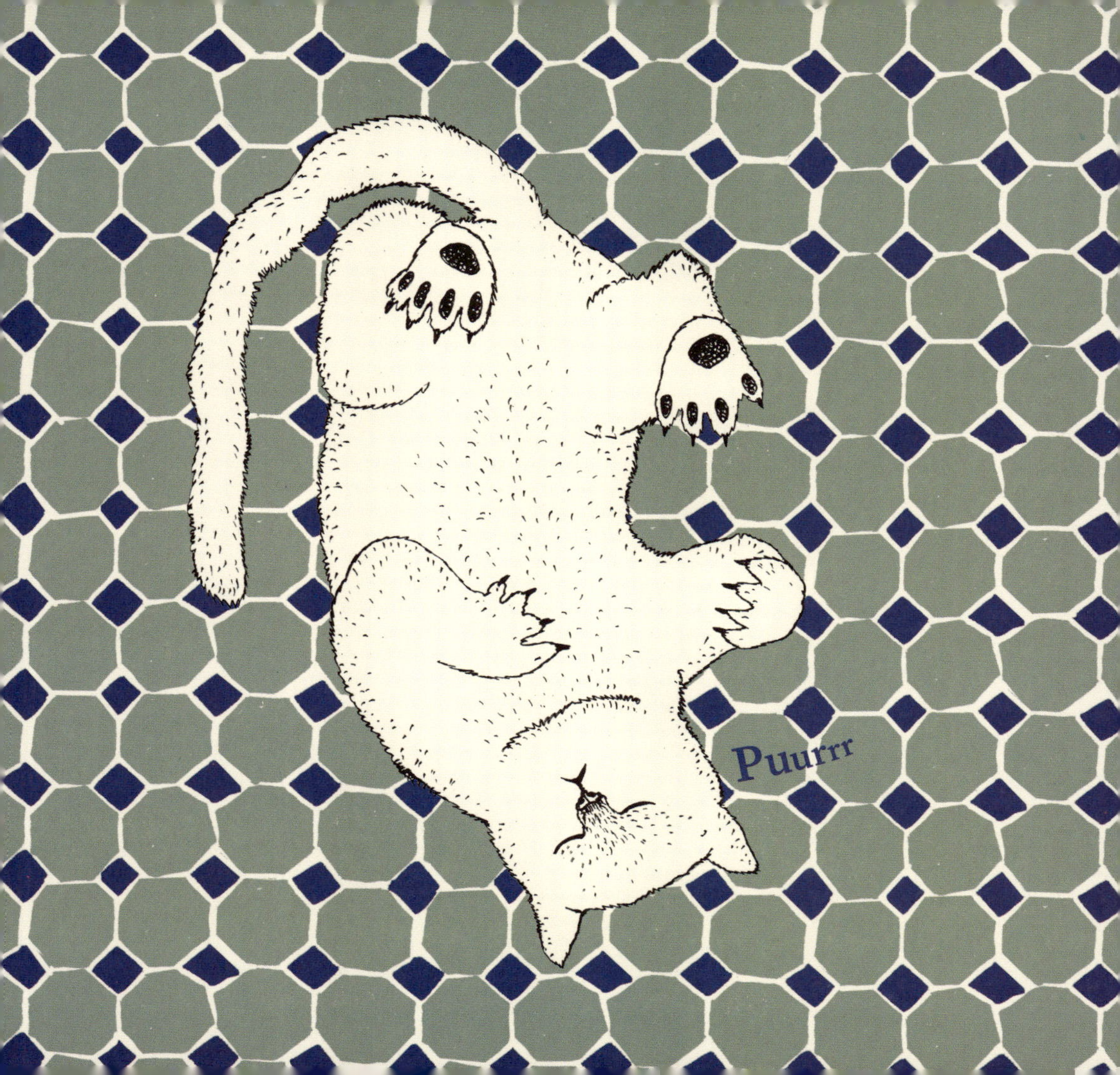
Puurrr

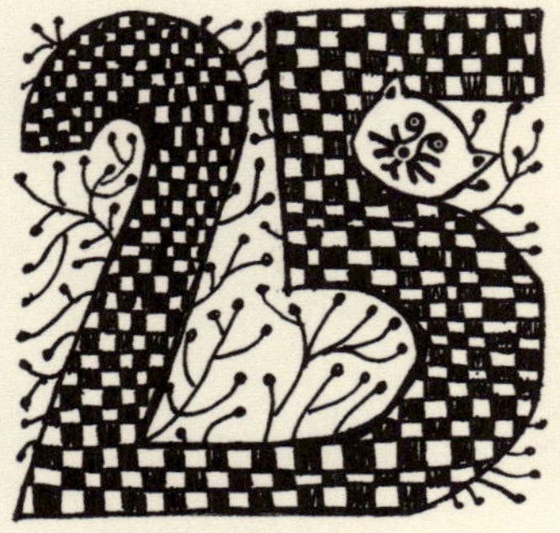

Bit of a chill in the air today,
Winter is setting in.
I must find a cosier spot to stay...
Ha! I've just found the very thing.
This woolly blanket will do the trick
And warm me up super-quick!
Purrr... purrr... purrr...

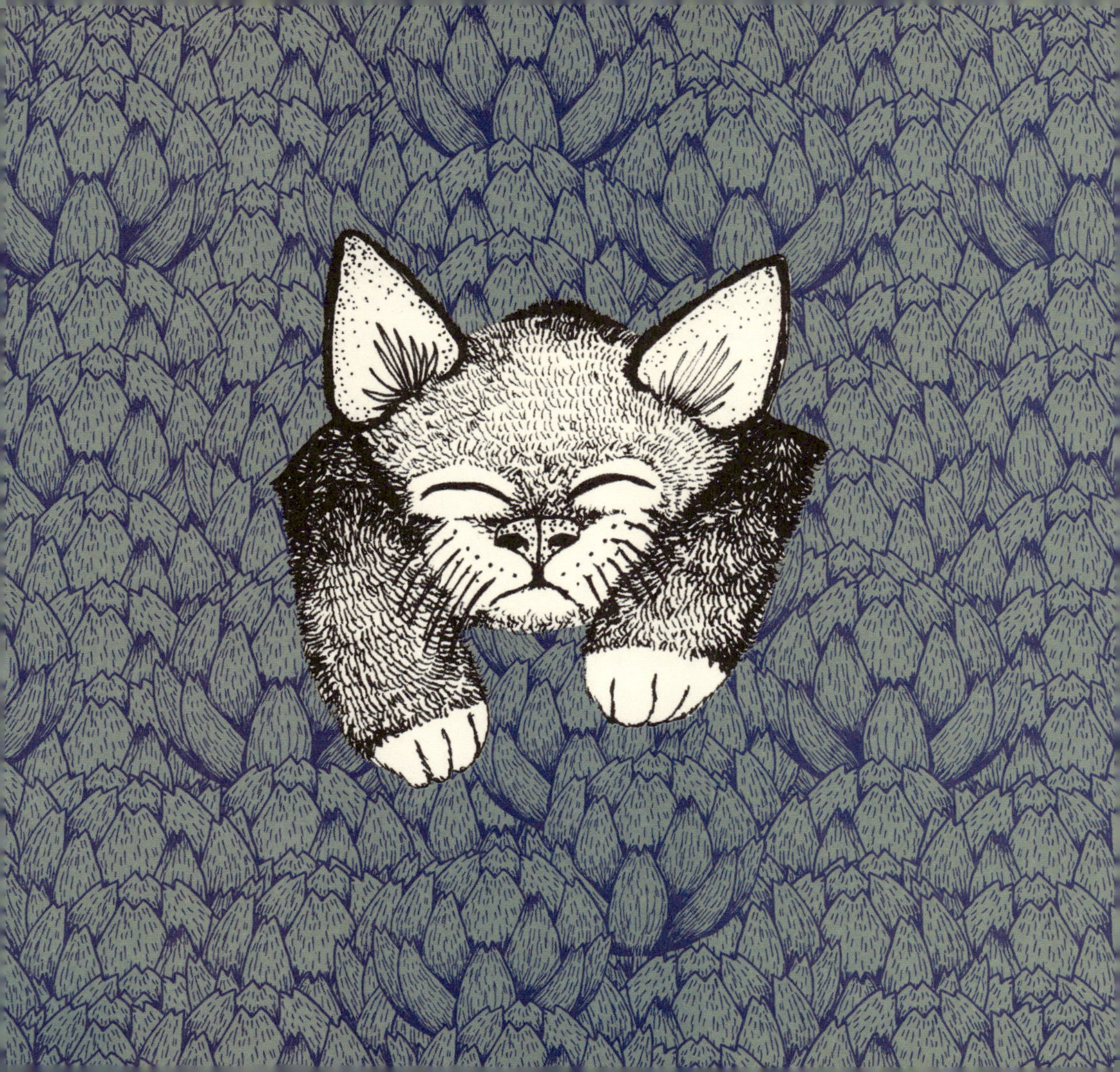

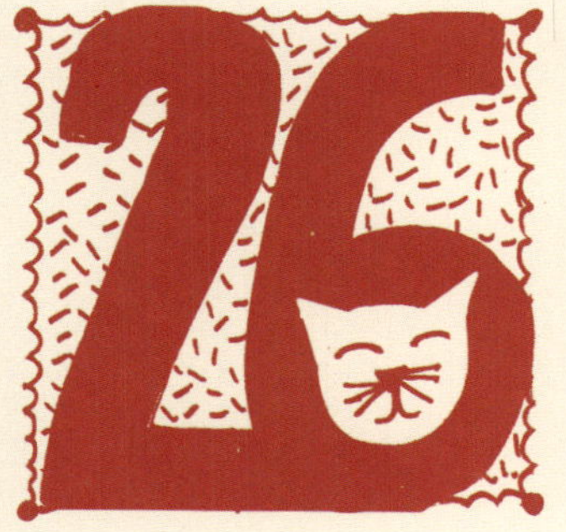

A soft feather cushion is perfect for me,
To relax and get on with some dreaming.
It's so much easier for me, you see,
To chase after birds while I'm sleeping!

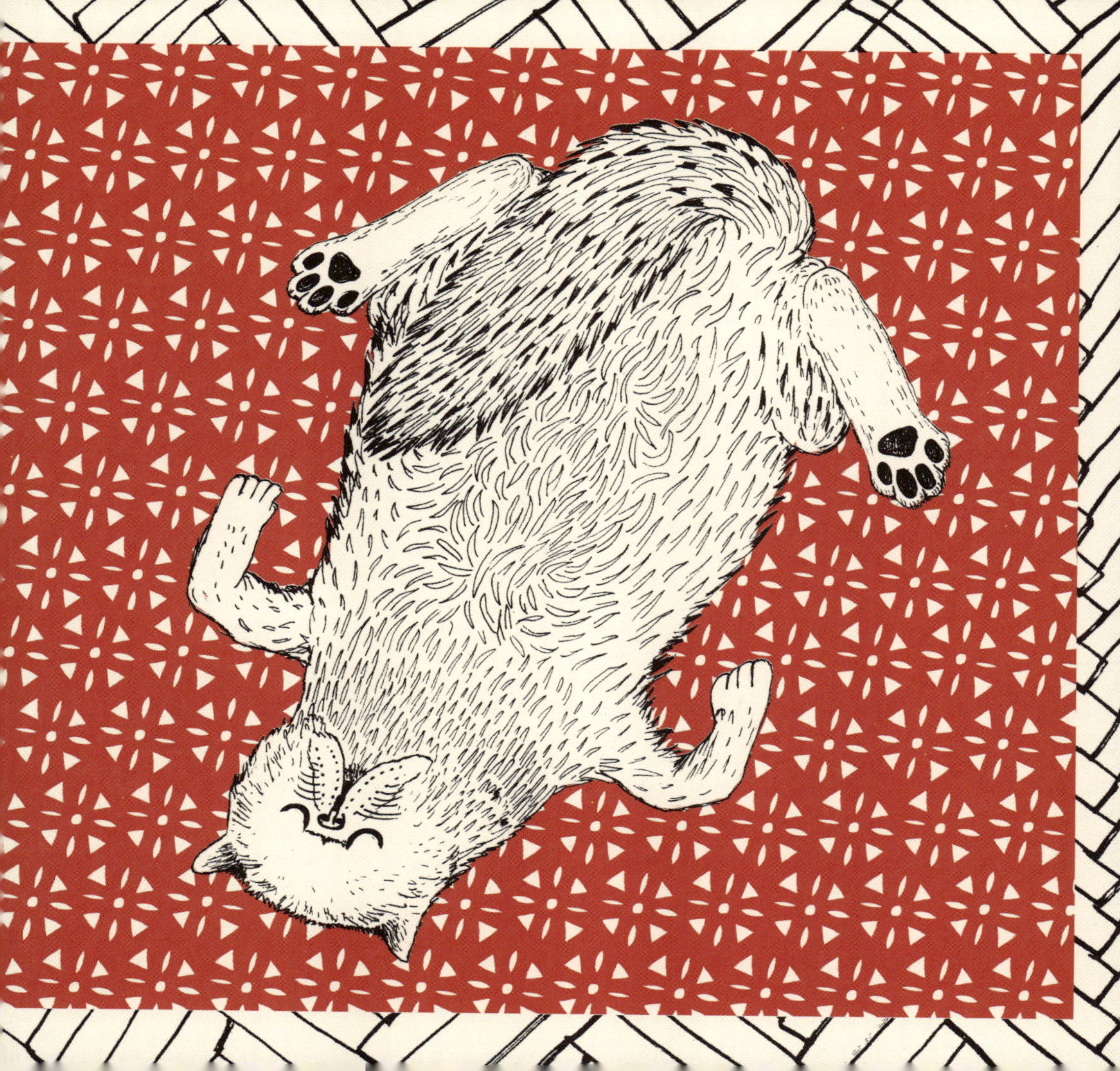

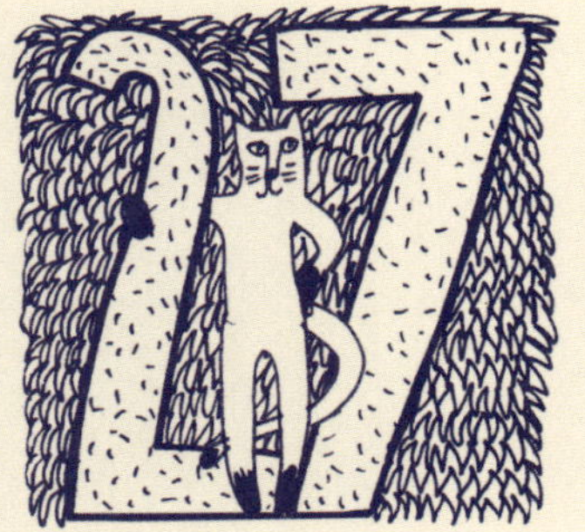

This cat looks beguiling,
No wonder he's smiling...
Having the perfect dream?
He's purring like mad,
Looks anything but sad...
He looks like the cat
That got all the cream.

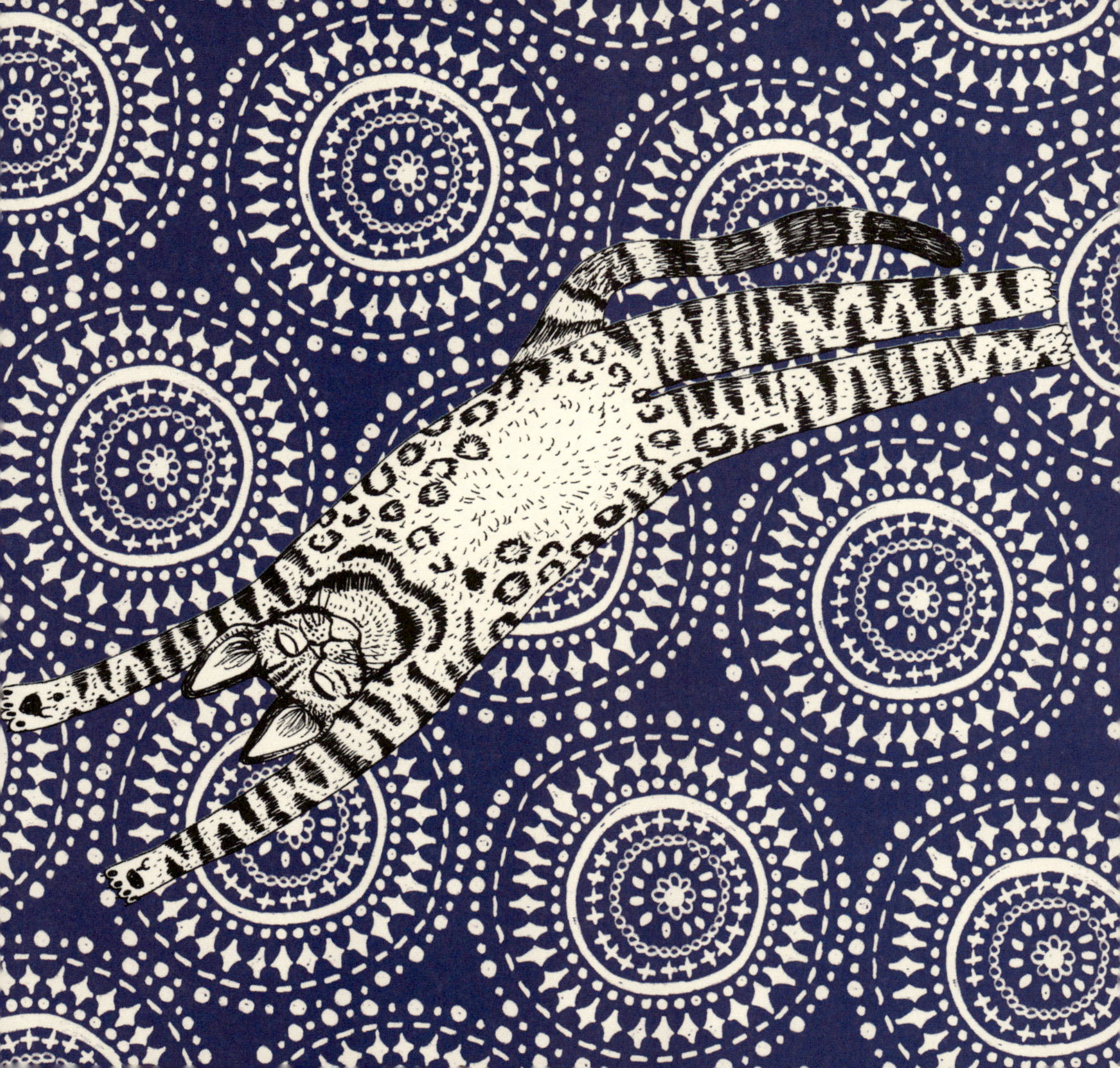

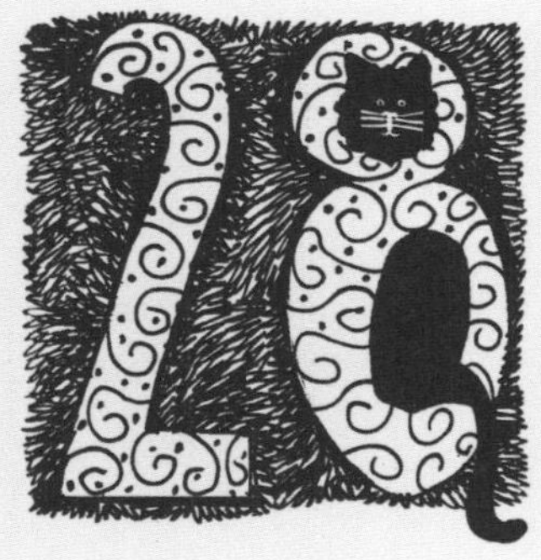

My sleeping spot is PRIVATE, y'know,
I wish you'd go away!
I can't relax and snooze, y'know,
If you're determined to stay.
Hmmmmph!

Are you still there?

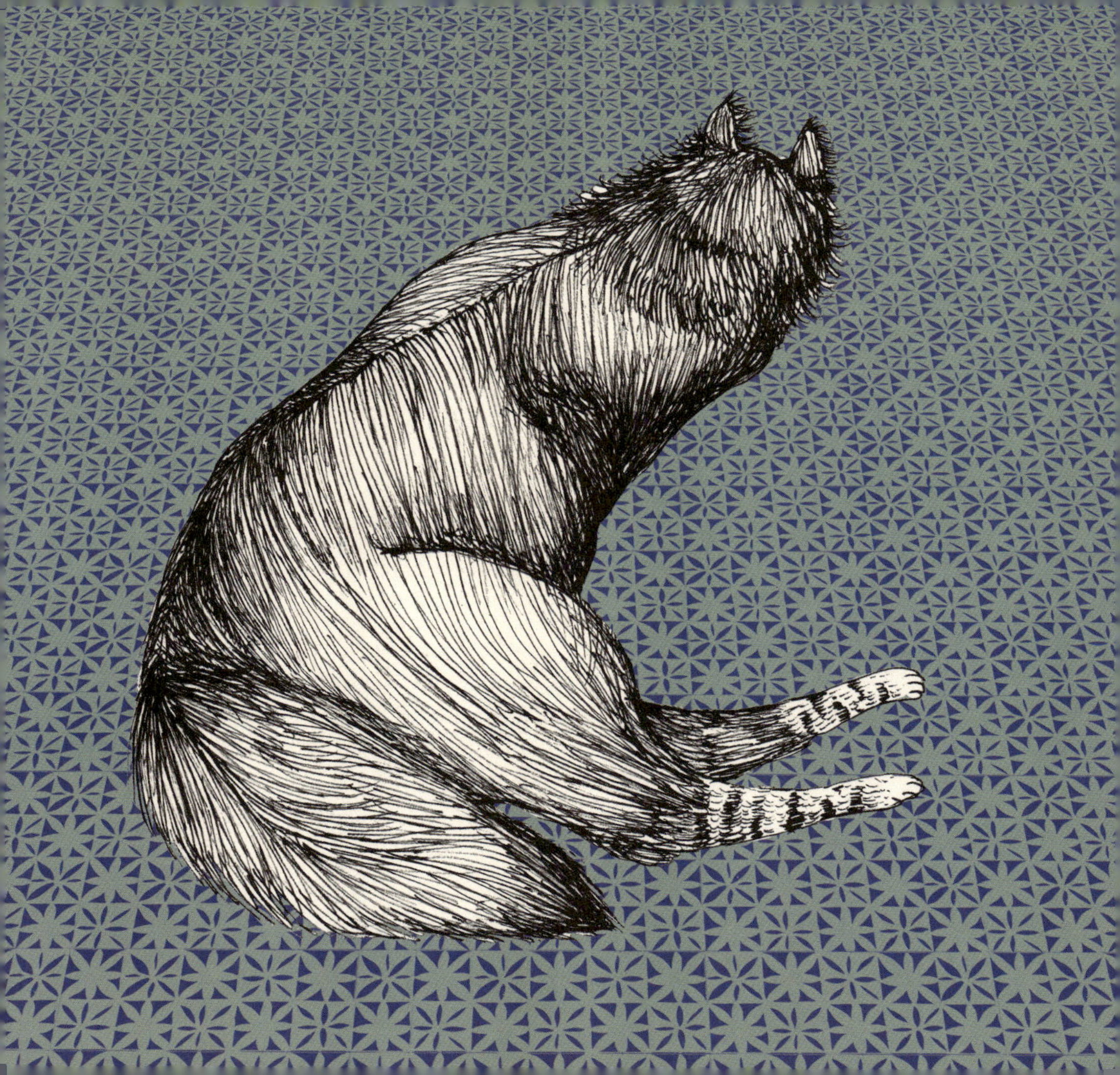

Whilst having a nap,
This cat needs a map,
As he's always on the move.
First his paws go East,
And then they go West,
Soon he'll have left the room!

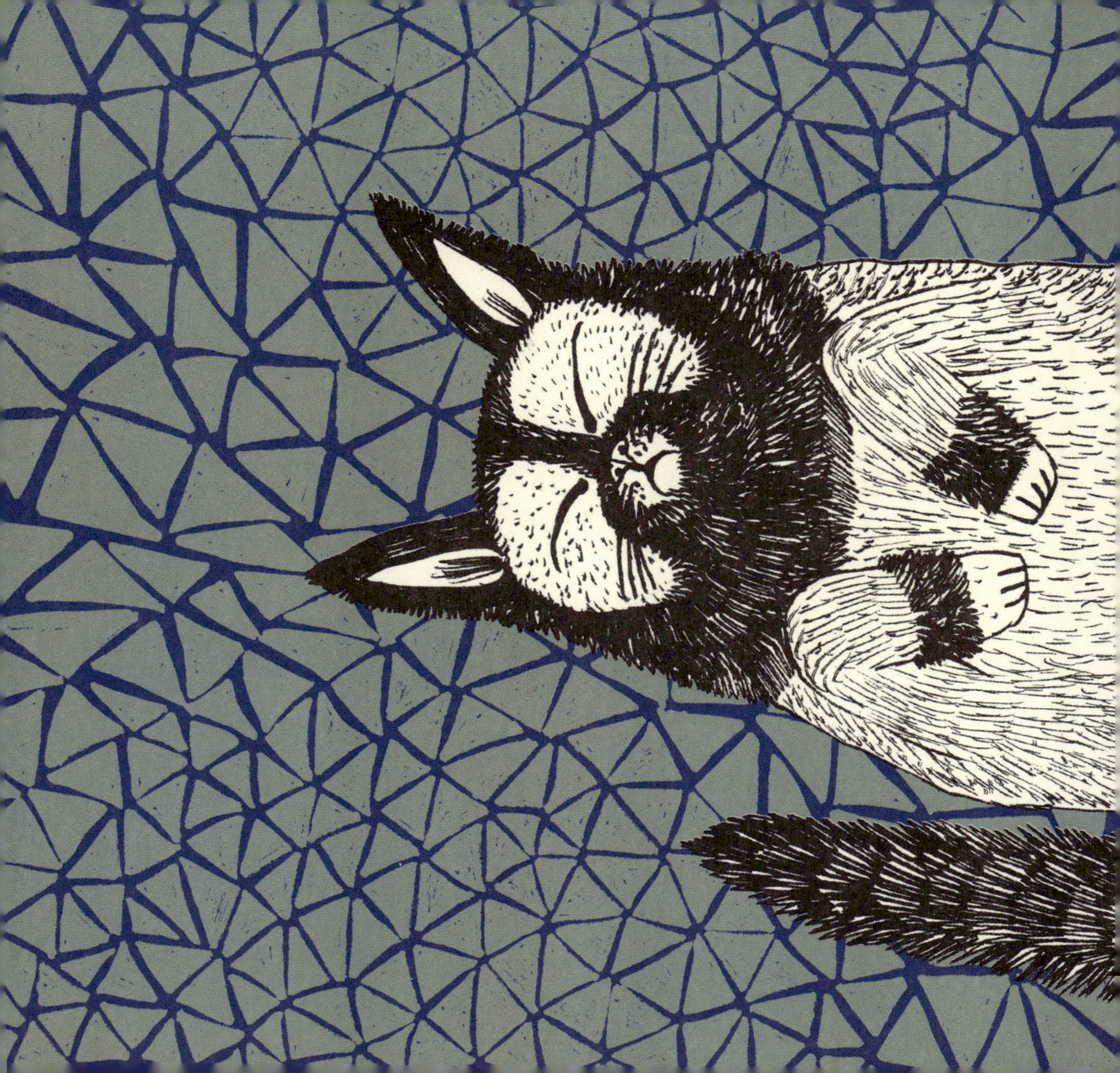

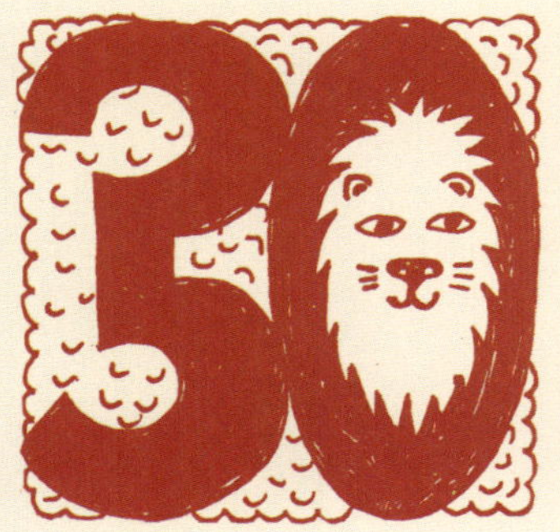

He's very young – a learner,
Seeing lots of ways to sleep.
He's noting all the poses,
But the learning curve is steep!
His brain is overheating,
In need of some repose.
He simply topples over
And falls into a doze.
Zzzzzz!

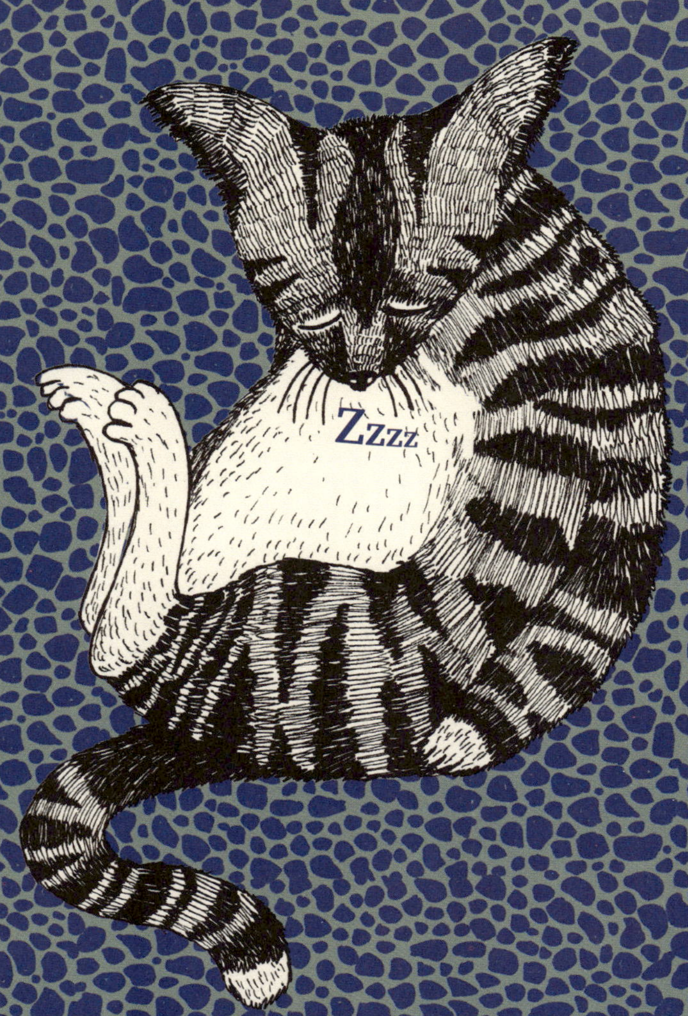
Zzzz

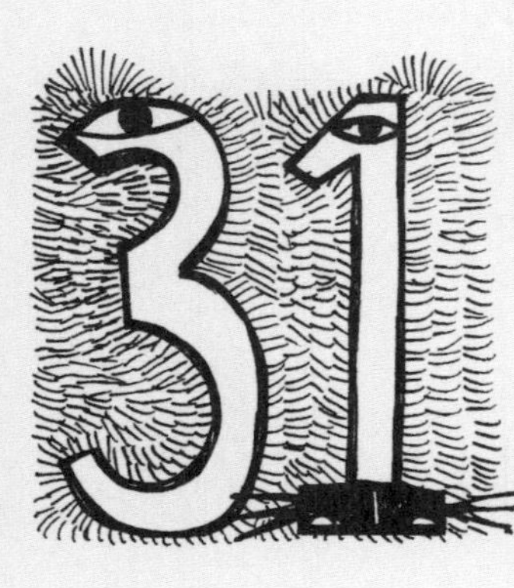

My mother's advice
Was 'Keep yourself nice.'
So... I like to look neat,
Even when I'm asleep.
My head rests on my paws –
Of course, no sign of claws.
And my toes I keep neatly pointed.
It's the best I can do so...
I hope you're not disappointed!

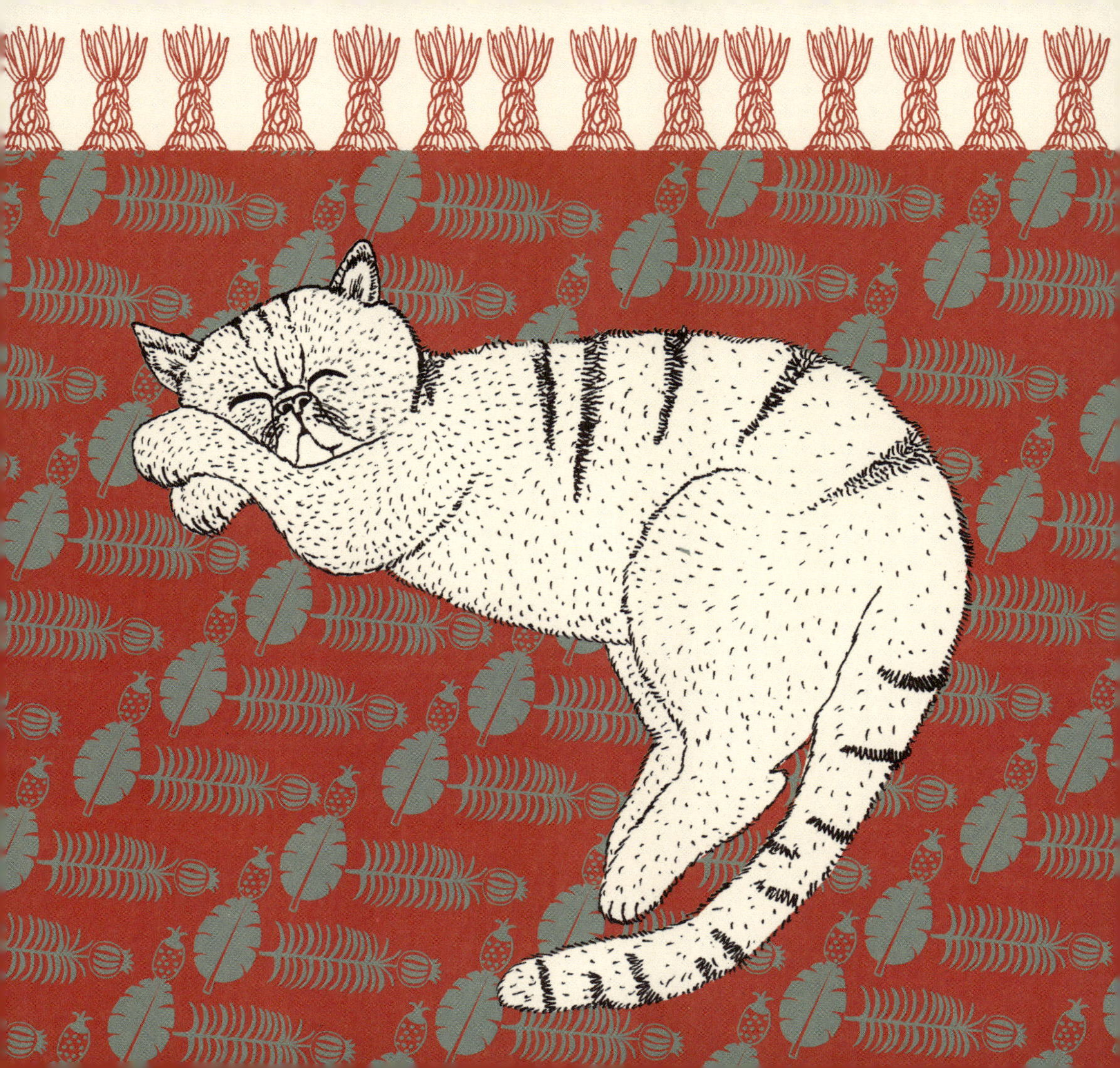

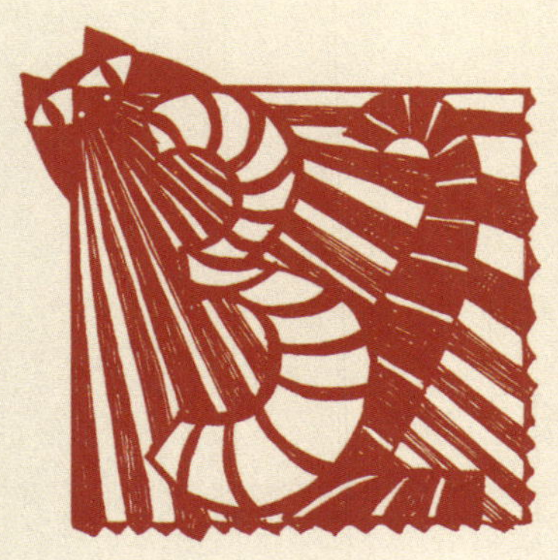

'Such a pretty cat,' they say,
  So one has to keep up standards.
'So, so sweet when asleep,' they say,
  'So unlike her brother, Bernard!'
    But this elegant pose, tho' nobody knows,
  Takes me ever so long to compose.

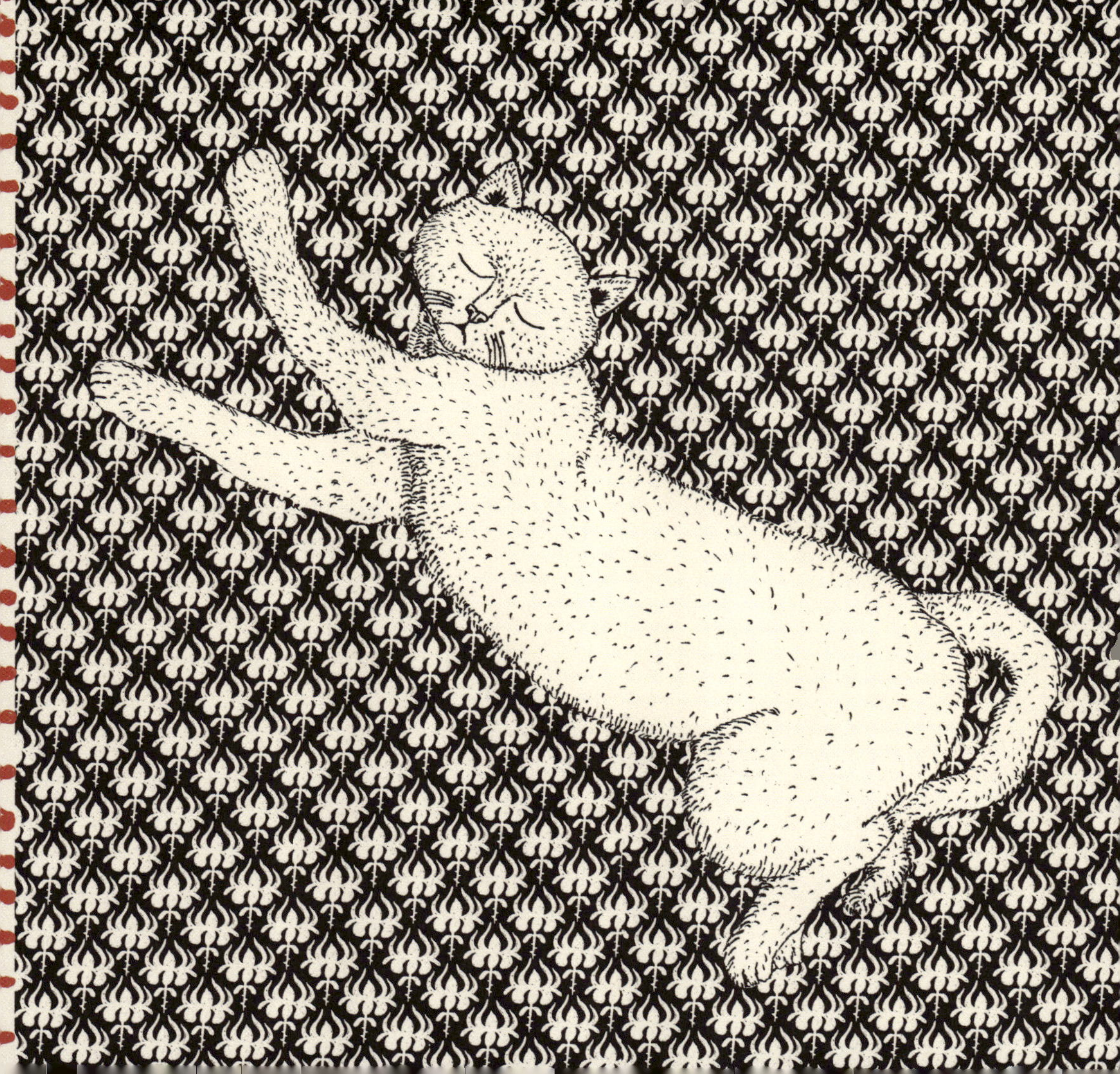

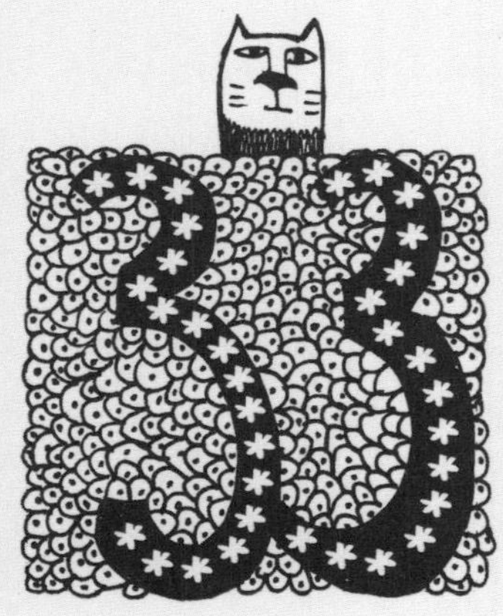

I'm so very fond of my master, y'know,
And he's so fond of me.
We've found the perfect way, y'know,
To share some time each day.
This catnapping spot is fab, y'know,
And the views are never, ever drab!

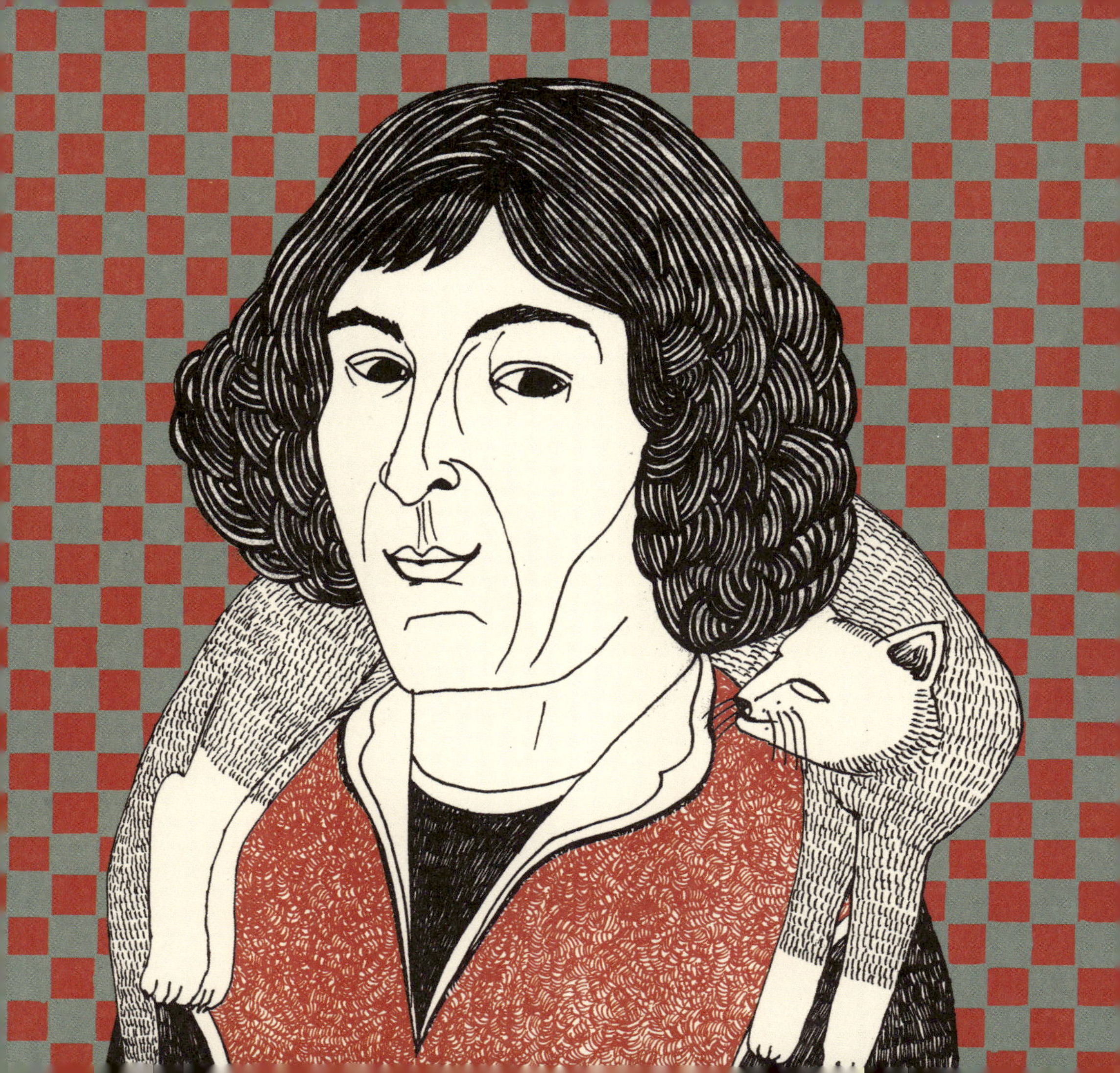

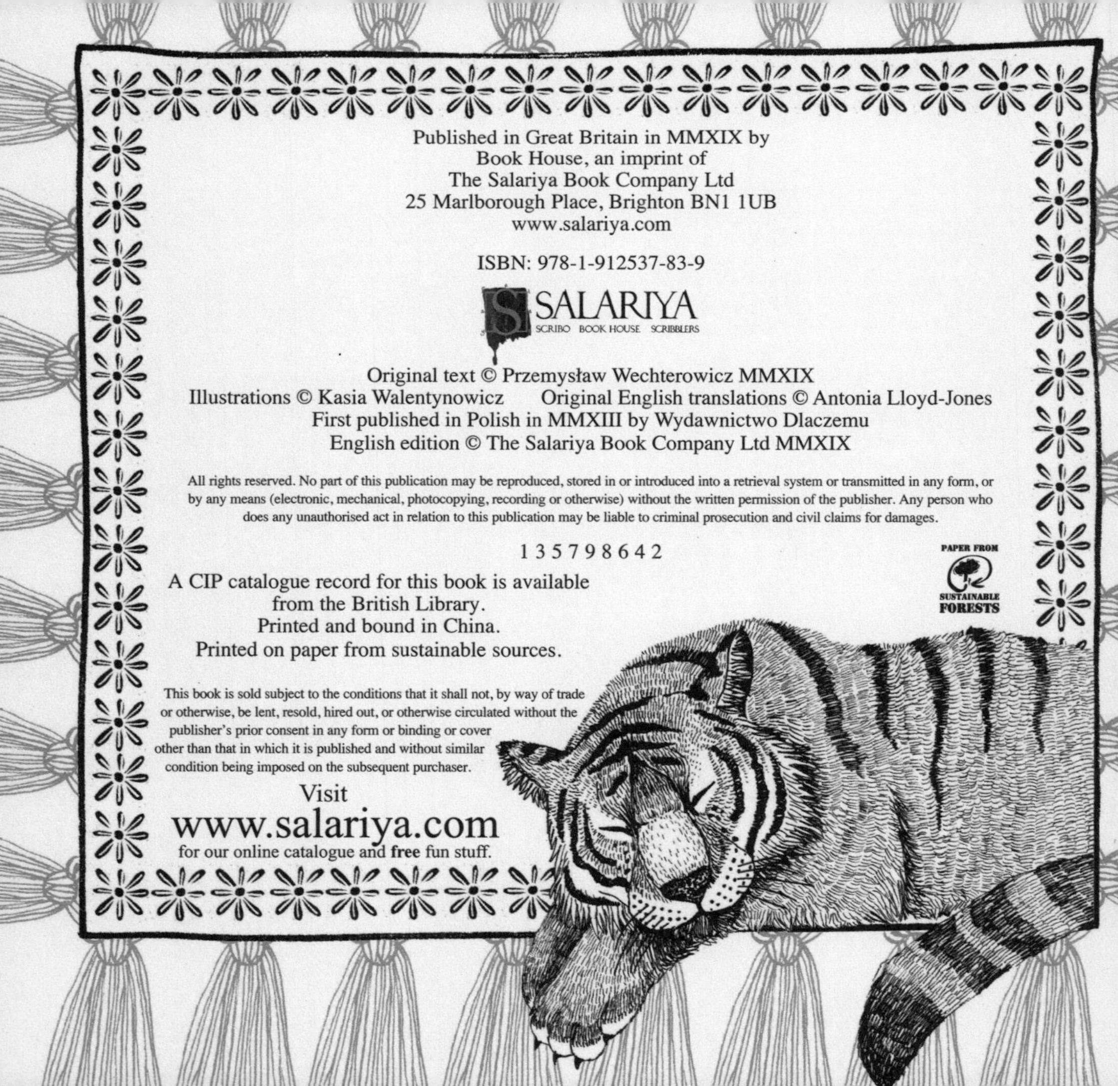

Published in Great Britain in MMXIX by
Book House, an imprint of
The Salariya Book Company Ltd
25 Marlborough Place, Brighton BN1 1UB
www.salariya.com

ISBN: 978-1-912537-83-9

SALARIYA
SCRIBO   BOOK HOUSE   SCRIBBLERS

Original text © Przemysław Wechterowicz MMXIX
Illustrations © Kasia Walentynowicz   Original English translations © Antonia Lloyd-Jones
First published in Polish in MMXIII by Wydawnictwo Dlaczemu
English edition © The Salariya Book Company Ltd MMXIX

1 3 5 7 9 8 6 4 2

PAPER FROM
SUSTAINABLE
FORESTS

A CIP catalogue record for this book is available
from the British Library.
Printed and bound in China.
Printed on paper from sustainable sources.

Visit
www.salariya.com
for our online catalogue and **free** fun stuff.

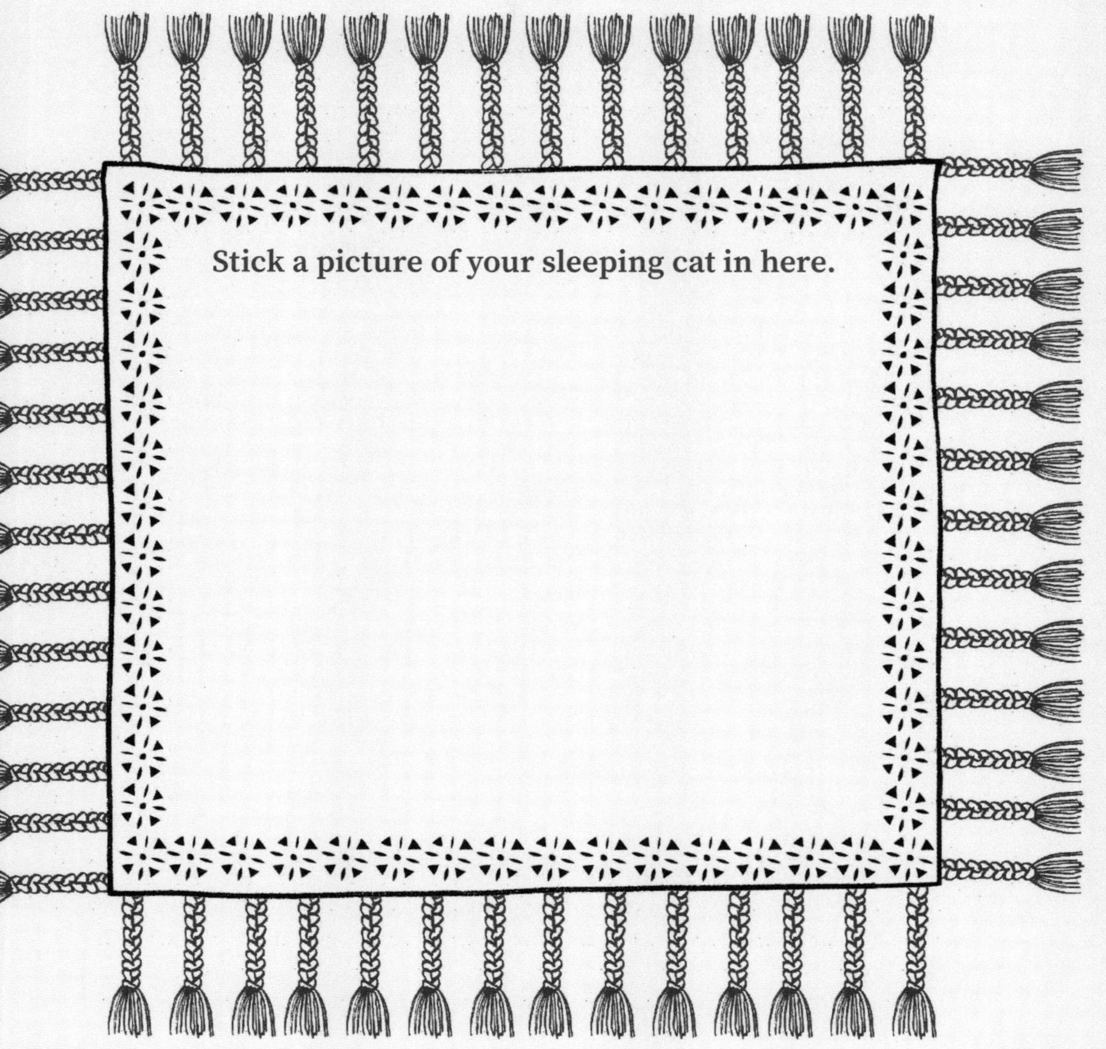

Stick a picture of your sleeping cat in here.

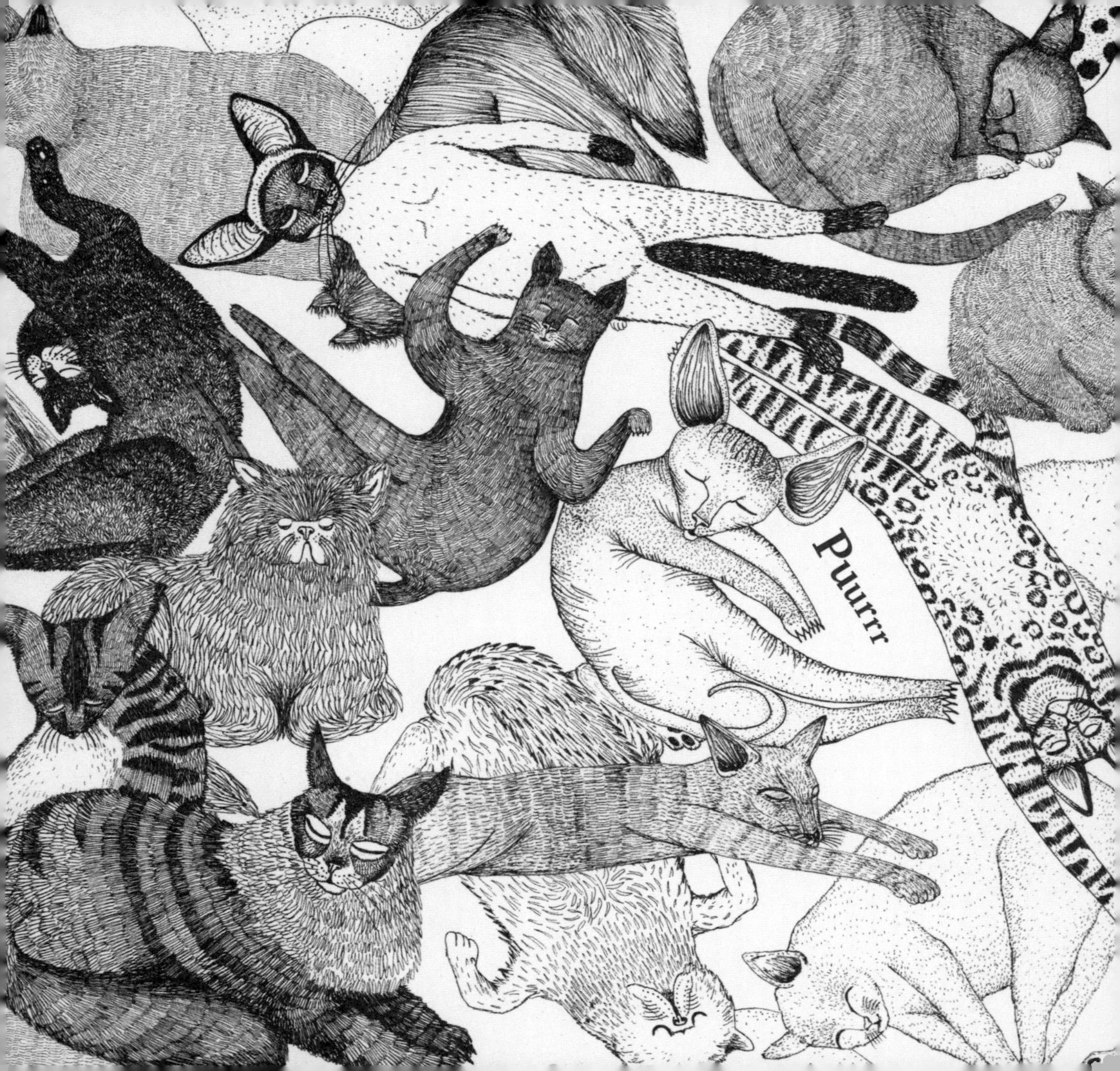
Puurrr